What a Husband Needs from His Wife

Physically | Emotionally | Spiritually

Melanie Chitwood

HARVEST HOUSE PUBLISHERS

EUGENE, OREGON

Backcover author photo © Judi Galusha

Cover by Left Coast Design, Portland, Oregon

Cover photo © Blend Images Photography/Veer

This book includes stories in which the author has changed some people's names and some details of their situations to protect their privacy.

WHAT A HUSBAND NEEDS FROM HIS WIFE
Copyright © 2006 by Melanie Chitwood
Published by Harvest House Publishers
Eugene, Oregon 97402
www.harvesthousepublishers.com

Library of Congress Cataloging-in-Publication Data
 Chitwood, Melanie, 1963-
 What a husband needs from his wife / Melanie Chitwood.
    p. cm.
  ISBN 978-0-7369-1830-5 (pbk.)
  1. Wives—Religious life. 2. Marriage—Religious aspects—Christianity. I. Title.
  BV4528.15.C45 2006
  248.8'435—dc22   2006001342

Printed in the United States of America

09 10 11 12 13 14 15 / BP-CF / 12 11 10 9 8 7 6

Readers' praise for
What a Husband Needs from His Wife

"God has used your book to transform my mind, my thinking, and my heart. It is nothing short of a miracle that God has made such major changes so quickly. My husband and I are reaping so many benefits. We are experiencing each other anew and enjoying just being together."

"Your book has changed my life. We were very close to divorce, but I credit your book with changing my whole perspective enough to save our marriage."

"No matter how long a couple has been married, newlyweds or married 52 years like us, they can benefit from the biblical and practical ideas in *What a Husband Needs from His Wife*."

"The very situations I have struggled with for years were addressed in *What a Husband Needs from His Wife*. As I have prayed and applied the principles in your book, I am seeing my marriage transformed right before my very eyes."

"Your book came into my life in God's perfect timing. I have highlighted, underlined, and circled so many words throughout the book. It has been like you wrote the book for me."

"This book is not a suggestion for a quick-fix formula to marital bliss. Instead, it is filled with real-life stories of victories and failures beyond the honeymoon."

"After reading *What a Husband Needs from His Wife*, a deep, unconditional love for my husband has overtaken me. For the first time during our marriage, instead of telling God about all my husband's faults, I have begun to thank the Lord for my mate, and I have asked God to change my faults. Miraculously, we now have the same love and affection that we had when we were dating."

"I am leading a Bible study through your book, and I see God working through this book in amazing ways. Many of the ladies have shared that their husbands notice positive changes in them, and one lady has even reconciled with her husband."

"It has taken your book to hit me over the head and to make me realize what a great husband I have."

"The main idea I've taken away from your book is that putting God first and seeking Him wholeheartedly is the best way to have a better marriage."

Contents

A Note from the Author

When you first read the title of this book, *What a Husband Needs from His Wife*, what came to your mind? I asked several women what they thought, and I received a variety of answers:

"I have no idea."

"I know what he thinks he needs: sex, sex, sex!"

"I've been trying to figure that out for a long time."

"I'll tell you exactly what my husband needs—a book on what a wife needs!"

I can understand and relate to all these responses, for I spent many years with little understanding of God's plan for me as a wife. *How could that have happened?* I wondered. *I've been a Christian for a long time and married much of that time.*

I sadly realized that I'd spent years trying to figure out marriage on my own strength and doing marriage my own way. In fact, I'd spent a whole lot of years telling my husband what he needed to do instead of focusing on what I needed to do. I remember hearing a man half-jokingly say something I could unfortunately relate to: "I didn't know what I thought till I got married and my wife told me!"

When I surrendered my marriage to God, He began a work of transformation in me and in my marriage. My marriage is now closer to what I want it to be and what most women long for—it's filled with peace, friendship, unity, intimacy, and joy. Like you, I am a work in progress, so with you I am still learning and growing in my marriage. I hope that as I share the journey of my marriage and the stories of other women, you will be encouraged to believe that you and your marriage can change too.

I believe what a husband needs from his wife is not a woman who just keeps trying harder to figure out marriage. Instead, a husband needs a woman who loves God, abides in Christ, and follows Him all the days of her life. This book does not reveal "ten easy steps to become the wife your husband needs." Instead, it is about having an ongoing personal relationship with Jesus Christ. *God* is the one who will change you and your marriage. He wants you to put your faith in Him, not in a self-improvement plan.

I hope you'll join me as you read the pages of this book with an open heart, an open mind, and a readiness to apply God's ways to your marriage. After reading about a specific biblical principle, ask God to show you how to live out that principle in your relationship with your husband. God's truths never change, but their applications to our marriages may vary.

I encourage you to look up every Scripture passage, both in the chapters and the study guide. Every word in the Bible is a word from God, and His Word is our instruction manual in marriage. Test the words I've written to make sure they line up with God's truth, for He is the One who can hold your marriage together and give you the kind of marriage you long for.

1

Pour Out Your Heart to God

While I was in an airport recently, I noticed a couple who were probably in their seventies, and they were obviously running late for their plane, feeling anxious and pressured to make it to their gate on time. They had mounds of luggage slowing them down, and the wife seemed to think they'd gain some time if she screeched at her husband. "Bill! Can't you see I can't carry all this? You need to get back here and get some of this luggage from me!" He forged on, weighed down by four bags of his own. She continued screeching at the top of her lungs all the way through security and then to the gate, which thankfully was a different one from mine. This was certainly not her finest moment. But then sadly, I thought, this was probably a typical moment for her.

I noticed another older couple at the airport that day, probably in their eighties. They stood out because of their complete contrast to the first couple. The husband was seated in a chair at our gate, and his wife was in a wheelchair. She obviously could not hear well, for each time her husband spoke to her, he slowly got up from his own seat and whispered into her ear. He gently touched her, looked into her eyes, and patiently waited for her response. Often her response was simply a sweet smile lighting up her face. Satisfied with that, he would sit down until the next time she needed him. I smiled inside, noticing how patient and tender they were with each other. I couldn't help but think, *I hope Scott and I are like that when we're their age.*

Have you ever imagined what your marriage will be like many years from now? Observing these couples in the airport triggered some dreams of what Scott and I will become in our old age. I realize that who we become as a married couple depends in many ways on how we are treating each other right now. The woman screeching at her husband at the airport did not become that way overnight. Likewise, the habits of the sweeter older couple were products of years of loving actions. As I reflect on my own marriage, I see that in some ways Scott and I have the kind of marriage we want, but in other ways we need God's transformation.

What thoughts do you have right now about your marriage and your husband? Maybe nothing is really wrong with your marriage. Maybe it's "just fine," but deep down inside you sense God has more planned for you and your husband. Or perhaps you're one of those women who can truly say her marriage is great. Thank God! I hope this book will encourage you to continue growing in your relationship with your husband.

Maybe you're weary from constant fighting but confused about how to get to a better place. Maybe you've tried and tried to make things better but have given up and lost all hope. Or worse, is your marriage in such a bad state that you don't really want to think about how to make it better?

Let me assure you that I can relate to whatever thoughts you've had about your marriage. As you read these pages, I want you to know they are written by someone who does not have marriage all figured out. In fact, when I called my husband (a pilot) to tell him the topic I was writing on, I made sure his plane was on the ground. I didn't want his laughter to cause a crash!

Pour Out Your Heart to God

I have often poured out my heart to God, praying for a marriage filled with less fighting and more peace, security, joy, fun, and intimacy. I knew God wanted my marriage to be different, but I wasn't sure how to get where God wanted me to be. I seemed to be growing in spiritual maturity in many areas of my life but not in my marriage. I prayed honestly and sincerely, *Lord, I'm weary with the way things are between me and Scott. After so many years, Lord, why is marriage so hard? Shouldn't it be getting easier? What do you want me to do?*

This time I got an unexpected response. My answer came as I was reading a very familiar verse and a specific word leaped out at me. Genesis 2:18 says, "The LORD God said, 'It is not good for the man to be alone. I will make him a helper suitable for him.'"

The word *helper* really caught my attention. I asked myself, *Am I being my husband's helper?* I felt such conviction that morning as I realized that more often than not, I expected Scott to be *my* helper. Of course, for a marriage to work we need to help each other, but God challenged me to examine my own behavior and to look at my marriage through His eyes.

That day became the start of a new journey for me, a journey that began with my willingness to turn away from my own way of doing marriage and turn to God's ways instead. God seemed to be piercing my heart with penetrating questions:

Was I willing to repent of the sin of doing marriage in my own strength and applying God's Word only when it suited me?

Did I just want to continue in my own stubborn ways, getting the same unsatisfying results in my marriage?

Did I trust God with all parts of my life, including my marriage?

Was I willing to stop telling my husband what he needed, and instead ask God what my husband needed?

Are you willing to honestly answer those same questions? Are you willing to let God's truth penetrate your heart? I encourage you now to stop reading, spend some time praying, and answer those questions honestly with God.

But Wait...

I hope you answered a resounding *yes!* Yes, Lord, I'm ready to look at my marriage from Your perspective and do things Your way. Yes, Lord, I'm ready to know and to follow Your plans for me as a wife. Yes, Lord, I'm ready to walk by faith and not by sight in my marriage.

However, if you're like me and many of the women I've talked to as I've been writing this book, you will have some reservations about discovering what your husband needs from you.

You might think the ideas in this book are outdated or overly traditional. You might believe that a woman who is dedicated to knowing what her husband needs is a woman who has neither a mind nor an identity of her own. One woman laughed out loud at the title of this book. Another said she would probably never read it. Still another woman said the title makes her think of hired help, like the housekeeper or gardener.

I discovered that many times a husband's needs are the last thing women want to talk about. After all, our pop culture promotes thoughts like these: *What about my needs? How can I be happy? How's this working for me? What's a quick fix?* However, considering that half of all marriages end in divorce, even among Christians, I would venture to say that our faulty thinking and practices are simply not working. Many women have adopted the lies of the world that tell them to put themselves first, fearing that if they don't, their husbands will take advantage of them.

I hope this book will point your heart and mind to God. God created marriage, and the Bible is His instruction manual. His Word is eternal and does not have an expiration date. Don't let Satan's lies rob you of discovering the treasure of a marriage lived God's way.

A second reservation might surface as you consider the challenges of your own marriage. Perhaps you're thinking, *But wait! You don't know what kind of marriage I'm in! You don't know what a jerk my husband can be! You don't know all the awful things he's said and done to me! He doesn't deserve my love at all!* No, I don't know about your marriage, but be assured that God knows everything about you, your husband, and your marriage. Nothing is too difficult for Him. No situation is beyond His loving hands and healing touch. Can you take your eyes off your husband's faults and focus on God and on yourself?

Now is a good time to remind you that if you are married, then marriage is God's will for you. During the numerous fights that took place when Scott and I were navigating the rocky early years of marriage, I occasionally thought I might have married the wrong man. Fortunately for us, those thoughts didn't last very long.

Sadly, I know that you, dear reader, may be a married woman who has experienced so many trials, hardships, misunderstandings, and hurt in your marriage that you just can't imagine going on. Divorce seems the only escape.

Remember, however, that God sees your broken heart and can mend whatever has divided you and your husband. God does allow a woman out of marriage in certain situations, such as infidelity or abuse. However, many women have found reconciliation in seemingly hopeless situations. If you are considering divorce, I encourage you to find a godly counselor.

I also want to remind you that if you have been divorced before, nothing can separate you from God's love. His compassion and mercy are new every morning.

One other reservation might be quietly hidden in the deep recesses of your mind and heart. It's the reservation of fear. Sometimes we don't ask God how to be the kind of wives our husbands need because we are afraid that following God's guidelines will cost us too much.

You will undoubtedly pay a price if you choose to follow God's ways. The price you'll pay is death to doing things your own way. But that's what being a Christian is about.

Philippians 2:3-4 shows us the way God asks us to live, a sacrificial life modeled by Christ:

> Do nothing from selfishness or empty conceit,
> but with humility of mind regard one another as more
> important than yourselves; do not merely look out for

your own personal interests, but also for the interests of others. Have this attitude in yourselves which was also in Christ Jesus, who, although He existed in the form of God, did not regard equality with God a thing to be grasped, but emptied Himself, taking the form of a bond-servant, and being made in the likeness of men. Being found in appearance as a man, He humbled Himself by becoming obedient to the point of death, even death on a cross.

Yes, we pay a price when we follow God's ways in our marriage, but the benefits in our relationship with Christ and our relationship with our husbands far surpass the cost.

Surrender Your Marriage

Maybe you're thinking to yourself that you already have a godly marriage and really don't need to change anything. Well, consider this question honestly and prayerfully: Have you surrendered your marriage to Christ? Are you doing some things in your marriage God's way but some your own way?

When I asked myself that question, I had a "lightbulb" moment. God clearly revealed to me that, yes, I had released to His lordship some areas of my life, even some areas of my marriage, but in other areas I held tight to my own ways. I was sprinkling into the recipe of my marriage a little bit of God and a whopping serving of me.

Women can be strong, efficient, and independent, but sometimes our self-reliance can wear us out and blind us to God's plan. Many women today might say, "I am woman, I am invincible, I am tired!" We think, *Be a good wife? Sure; I can do that! I'll clean the house, iron my husband's clothes, and put a smile on my face. Be a good Christian? Sure! I'll serve in women's ministry and children's ministry, and I'll fix meals for those in need. Be a good mom? Sure! My children will be obedient and happy. Help with the family finances? I can squeeze a career in here somewhere! And I'll try to be cute and fit while I'm at it!* And on and on our efforts continue until, like the little hamster on his exercise wheel, we have worn ourselves out and gotten nowhere.

Sometimes we have to get to the end of ourselves before we turn to God. Brokenness hurts, but when we're broken we're more likely to admit that apart from Christ we can do nothing (John 15:5).

Writer Anabel Gillham describes in her book *The Confident Woman: Knowing Who You Are in Christ* the moment she surrendered her marriage to God's hands:

> I had gone to bed. It had been a bad day. I don't remember why—I had a lot of bad days. I was sobbing, praying, "God, I don't understand what is going on in my life. My marriage is so far away from what I long for it to be; my kids are not turning out the way I want them to. And I'm so tired. I've given, given, and given, and I don't think I can give anymore. I have made one grand mess of everything."
>
> Then I said what I had never said in all my 40-some-odd years of life: "I give up. I have failed. *I can't do it.* If anything is going to come out of this marriage and these kids, if anything is going to come out of this life, You're going to have to do it, because I can't."…I believe God spoke to me that night in the quiet of my bedroom. A thought came into my conscious awareness that was foreign to my way of thinking. It was a simple little phrase: "Thank you, Anabel, I will do it all *for you.*"[1]

Surrender is completely counter to our human nature, but this is right where God wants us to be. Sometimes I sense God saying to me through the whisper of the Holy Spirit on my heart or a verse that leaps from the pages of Scripture, *I am God and you are not. I am really good at being God. You are not. When you get out of the way, I can work.*

Surrendering is one way to say that we depend on God, not on ourselves and our own efforts. Even though we don't know what's around the corner, we put our marriage in the hands of the One who made us and loves us, trusting Him in whatever comes our way, good or bad.

How do we surrender our marriages to God? What exactly do we surrender?

First, we surrender our right to have marriage work the way we think it should. We give up feeling entitled to what we deserve in marriage. I came in to marriage thinking I deserved many things. I thought I deserved to be a stay-at-home mother while my husband provided for our family. I thought I deserved a certain level of comfort with a nice house and beautiful furnishings. Living a comfortable life included shopping for clothes and going to restaurants frequently. When I did not get what I thought I deserved, I was unhappy and moody and made my husband feel as if he were a failure.

Second, we surrender our expectations of our husbands. The main expectation I had of Scott was that he would make me happy. I expected him to know my needs and cater to them. When Scott and I first married, I was insecure about his love for me, so I made him prove his love all the time. I wanted him to prove his love by being home with me, by choosing me over other activities or people, by telling me he loved and appreciated me. These needs were not inherently bad, but I was draining Scott by turning to my husband to satisfy my longings. Of course, the only One who can meet our deepest needs is God. He is the one we go to with all of our needs. The more I went to Scott with these needs, the more he withdrew from my extreme dependency. In turn I felt as if Scott were failing me, and we were trapped in this unsatisfying cycle.

As I turned to God with a sincere heart, I knew that I had to confess to God all of the sins I had committed against Scott and consequently against God. I prayed that God would reveal the sins to me so I could confess them to Him and then be free of them. Seeing so much ugliness in my heart was hard as I confessed sins such as pride, judgment, self-pity, self-righteousness, anger, bitterness, unforgiveness, selfishness, manipulation, and rebellion. As I was honest with God, He reminded me that *while* I was still a sinner, Christ died for me (Romans 5:8). Jesus Christ has already paid the price for our sins. We confess our sins, accept His forgiveness, and repent. In Acts 3:19 Peter says, "Therefore repent and return, so that your sins may be wiped away, in order that times of refreshing may come from the presence of the Lord." God truly did refresh me and my marriage as I put my marriage in His loving hands.

Surrendering our marriages to God and repenting of our sins is an ongoing process. God wants us to be in constant fellowship with Him, seeking Him with our whole hearts through prayer, listening, reading His Word, and obeying Him.

Transformed by His Love

Many women I have talked to about the ideas of this book have a common denominator keeping them from surrendering completely to God: They do not believe in God's unconditional love.

You may say to yourself, *Well, I'm a Christian. Of course I believe God loves me.* Or you may wonder what accepting God's love has to do with surrendering. Let me share with you a revelation that really changed me.

As I began to be honest with God about my marriage, I started to realize that for a long time I had questioned God's unconditional love for me. I had always felt that I didn't quite measured up. I was good, but not good enough; pretty, but not pretty enough; smart, but not smart enough; a good mother, but not good enough. You fill in the blank—I was just not worthy of God's unconditional love. I knew God loved me, but I thought I could help Him love me even more if I did something to deserve His love. I finally sensed God saying, *Stop striving. Just receive the gift of My love for you. You're My child. I created you so I could love you and you could love Me.* God's unconditional love, so different from human love, is not dependent on anything about us. It's just who God is.

God wants us to get His love settled in our hearts for once and for all. He wants us to be absolutely sure we can never add to or subtract from His love. He loves us because we are His children. First John 4:16 tells us that we have to believe God loves us because God is love: "We have come to know and have believed the love which God has for us. God is love." Once we believe in God's unconditional and personal love, we can trust Him and surrender everything in our lives to Him, including our marriages. God's love will transform us, and we'll love our husbands out of the wellspring of love God has put in us by His Spirit.

I've said this before, but I want to repeat this reminder. As you read this book, be careful not to think of it as a self-improvement plan. Anything based on fixing or changing our marriages in our own strength is missing the point. A self-improvement plan focuses on self. By surrendering our marriages, however, we are putting our faith in God. As you read numerous ideas to apply to your marriage, ask the Holy Spirit to show which specific actions and attitudes your husband needs, and ask God to reveal ideas not mentioned here. God knows you and your husband. He knows the transformation your marriage needs.

Remember that transformation is God's work, not yours. Your part is to surrender, confess, submit to His principles for a godly wife, and obey. As this transformation takes place, it will reflect the kind of marriage He intended for you and your husband. Isaiah 43:18-19 is a reminder of the new life only God can bring to your marriage. "Do not call to mind the former things, or ponder things of the past. Behold, I will do something new, now it will spring forth; will you not be aware of it? I will even make a roadway in the wilderness, rivers in the desert."

An Everlasting Rock

If you've been married very long, you know that marriage has ups and downs, times of storms and times of bright sunshine. The storms in marriage include temptations, doubts, financial disasters, infidelity, miscarriage, problems with children, daily stresses of life, and sickness. Through the storms, God promises to be the Rock in our marriages. Scripture is filled with references to God as our Rock. "Trust in the LORD forever, for in God the LORD, we have an everlasting Rock" (Isaiah 26:4). Our Rock is a firm foundation during the storms that threaten our marriages.

In Matthew 7:24-25 God calls a man who builds his life on the Rock of Jesus Christ a wise man. A wise man can survive the storms of life: "And the rain fell, and the floods came, and the winds blew and slammed against the house; and yet it did not fall, for it had been founded on the rock." In contrast is the foolish man who built his house on the sand. When the storms came, "great was its fall" (Matthew 7:27). Are you wise or foolish as you build your marriage?

I like visual reminders of spiritual truths. A couple of years ago I was trying to think of a fun and different gift for my husband, Scott. We had been doing some landscaping, so I got the bright idea to get him a rock for the yard. Now, I'm a city girl who knows how to shop, so I directed my van to the landscape shop and for $69 bought a pretty big rock. My reason for getting the rock was certainly not spiritual; I was just trying to be creative. But since we've added that rock to our yard, I love sitting out front and watching the kids play, visiting with friends, or drinking a cup of coffee. The rock in our yard has become a reminder that Jesus is the Rock of our family.

A Fresh Perspective

When I surrendered my marriage to God, He gave me many fresh insights. He prompted me to begin looking at marriage from *His* perspective. Are you ready for a fresh perspective in your marriage?

As I write this, I'm enjoying the beginning of spring here in Charlotte, North Carolina. From this season God gave me a picture of how I've been treating my marriage.

Picture a large garden filled with tall weeds. Then picture yourself with a lawn mower—a big and powerful riding lawn mower. You steer your lawn mower toward the tallest weed and plow it down. You continue this until every weed is decimated. You wipe your hands and think to yourself, *Job well done.* Sure, the weeds will grow back, but you can just mow them down again.

Then your eye spots another garden in your yard. It's not as big as the first, but it's also filled with tall weeds. Time to power up the lawn mower again. But wait—there's already a gardener there. You can't see the gardener's face because it's covered with the brim of a hat. This gardener is working slowly and carefully. He yanks out each tall weed by hand and deposits it in a trash pile that's growing taller. *Well, that's certainly going to take a long time,* you think to yourself. *Maybe I should offer my lawn mower.* Then the gardener waves for you to come over. You slowly walk toward the garden, and as you draw closer you notice for the first time an array of beautiful and brilliantly colored flowers. They're small—just beginning to bloom—and had been hidden by the weeds.

God showed me that I was treating my marriage and its challenges like the first gardener. I was just plowing through, trying my own methods of fixing things and decimating everything in my path. And the improvements I made were just temporary. God said to me, *Let Me be the Gardener of your marriage. Let's try My gentle ways. I will help you uncover the precious treasures in your marriage.*

Are you ready to follow God's way more completely in your marriage? Are you ready to let God transform you and your marriage? If so, cooperate with Him by doing these three things: First, as you work through this book, keep a notebook. Write your responses to the things you read, the ideas that come to mind, and your hopes for your life and your marriage. Second, after you read a chapter, turn to the study guide at the back of the book and answer the questions there. Record yours answers in your notebook. And third, stop right now and talk honestly with God in prayer about your marriage. Remember to make seeking Jesus your goal. Use this prayer as a guide and speak honestly from your heart about anything that's keeping you from wanting to do marriage God's way. As you pray, you might want to open your hands and turn your palms upward to symbolize your surrender.

PRAYER GUIDE

Dear Lord,

Thank You for my husband and my marriage. I want the marriage You want me to have, Lord. I confess that I've tried to make it into what I want it to be, not necessarily what You want it to be. I surrender myself and my marriage into Your loving hands and Your sovereign lordship. Give me the desire and the strength to be the kind of wife You want me to be. Then I know I'll be the wife my husband needs. Amen.

2

Start with Jesus

~⁓~

Scott and I thought all our dreams were coming true six years ago when we moved to Charlotte, North Carolina, for Scott to begin work as a pilot for US Airways. We had a four-year-old son, Zachary, and a four-month-old son, Tyler, and for the first time I was a stay-at-home mom.

Although we didn't know a soul in Charlotte, we immediately found a great church and were confident in time we'd have some great friendships. And we did—but we also had some long, lonely days in between!

Pilots travel and are away from home many nights in a row, and Scott was no exception. At first our new life in Charlotte fueled my happiness, but gradually reality set in, and I did not handle it very well.

Babies and preschoolers have an amazing ability to wake up at the crack of dawn. With the day looming ahead of me, I would wonder,

What on earth am I going to do all day? I loved being with my sons, but I was starving for my husband's companionship and the friendship of other women.

Instead of turning to God, I let each long day of loneliness become a brick in the wall around my heart. I was bitter and hard-hearted toward Scott, resentful that he was away so much—even though he was away working and providing for his family. I was selfishly caught up in my own emotions. When Scott walked in the door after being gone for several days, instead of welcoming him home with open arms, I often walked out the door to go shopping. I wanted him to feel as miserable as I did.

One morning before Scott left for work, we had a huge fight. I don't remember the details, but I'm sure I was whining about something and didn't think Scott was responding the right way.

I had planned to attend a women's Bible study that morning, but after fighting with Scott I just didn't feel like going. I called my Bible study leader, Debbie, and tearfully told her I wouldn't be there because of the big fight I'd had with Scott. I added some juicy details, hoping to elicit her sympathy and understanding. I'll never forget her response. Debbie simply answered, "Melanie, just come to Bible study."

I told her I'd think about it and hung up the phone. Not only was I mad at Scott, but now I was a little miffed at Debbie for not empathizing more with me. I was a mess!

That day I did go to Bible study, and gradually I began to take my eyes off myself. Instead I began to focus my eyes on God. As I did, my marriage began to change.

Seek God First

Before we seek better marriages, God wants us to seek Him *first*. We can easily fall into the trap of thinking that we just need to try harder to have better marriages or to figure out what our husbands need. If that becomes our focus, then better marriages or even our husbands become our idols. But if we seek Jesus alone, He'll show us His ways for our marriages.

What does seeking God entail? When I think of seeking God, I think of searching with eagerness and longing. I think of putting all my energies into pursuing God.

The main way I seek God is through a daily quiet time. I made this a consistent practice when we first moved to Charlotte, and I can honestly say nothing has changed my relationship with God more than this.

I know that finding a quiet moment in your day can be hard. Certainly in some seasons in your life, such as when you have very small children, you will feel as if the only alone time you have is when you go to the bathroom—and even then those little ones will find you! However, it can be done. Think about things in your life that really matter to you. Do you find time for those? Of course you do. For most of us, time is not really the issue. We need to make a choice: Will we or will we not have a quiet time? Offering up a bunch of excuses for not having a quiet time is much easier than actually having one.

Jesus' example in Mark 1:35 offers a compelling reason to make a quiet time a priority. "In the early morning, while it was still dark, Jesus got up, left the house, and went away to a secluded place, and was praying there." Even Jesus, the Son of God, needed time alone with His Father. How could we possibly think we don't need the same?

What Is a Quiet Time?

A quiet time is simply a time you are still and alone with God to pray, listen, and read Scripture. You don't need to follow a formula, but some suggestions might be helpful. Let's begin with some practical considerations.

When should you have your quiet time? It's up to you. For me, before both our boys were in school, the best time proved to be early in the morning before anyone else was awake. I can just hear some of you saying, "But I'm not a morning person!" Well, neither was I, but I learned to be one! Other times in the day just didn't work for me. I would inevitably be interrupted or distracted or tired. I know many women who have numerous children or who work outside the home who have developed the practice of a morning quiet time. They just make this choice consistently, day after day.

Whatever time you choose, make this a daily habit so you can develop consistency. I've heard people say that we are what we repeatedly do. If I repeatedly put off time with God, I'll be a woman who has a very shallow relationship with God. If you're new to quiet times, start with a small amount of time, even if it's only five minutes. Gradually your time with God will become a time you won't miss for the world.

Be Still and Know

Another aspect of a quiet time is being still. Oh, that's hard! Being still in body and mind is a challenge, but it's something God commands us to do: "Be still, and know that I am God" (Psalm 46:10 NIV). To develop a closer relationship with God, we need a "sitting still and doing nothing else" time with God. Think of it this way: Would you rather have a conversation with your husband while he's working on the computer or while the two of you are sitting on the couch together with no other distractions?

When I return from taking my sons to school, the first thing I plan to do each morning is to have my quiet time. Immediately I'm faced with temptations leading me away from my number one priority of meeting with God. The news on TV or the Internet, e-mails, phone calls, and my to-do list tempt me to get busy. Satan does not want me to meet with the Lord. Satan will try to deceive me by making me think that the most important thing I can do is to be in motion.

The story of Jesus visiting Martha and Mary in their home pictures perfectly the priorities Jesus wants us to have. Mary is "seated at the Lord's feet, listening to His word" (Luke 10:39). Meanwhile Martha is running around, busy with her hostess responsibilities. Finally in frustration, Martha appeals to Jesus, hoping He will reprimand Mary. Instead, He admonishes Martha: "Martha, Martha, you are worried and bothered about so many things; but only one thing is necessary, for Mary has chosen the good part, which shall not be taken away from her" (Luke 10:41-42).

"The good part" is sitting at Jesus' feet. It's making our quiet time our number one priority. My pastor gave our congregation a lasting lesson on priorities with this visual illustration. He showed the congregation two large jars. In the first jar he placed large rocks until they reached the top of the jar. He then asked, "Is the jar full?" Most of the congregation answered yes. Then he poured sand into the jar, showing us that the jar had not been full after all. In the second jar he reversed the process. He first poured the sand into the jar. Next he tried to put the large rocks in, but of course, they would not fit. Do you see the lesson? We must put first things first, or we'll miss out on the most important thing, "the good part" of sitting at Jesus' feet.

When I'm on My Knees

Bending down with rag in hand, I wiped the coffee spills off the kitchen floor. Then my eye caught the spills dribbled down the cupboard door. *I'm surprised I haven't seen that before,* I thought to myself as I continued to clean. *Wow, there's more dog hair down here than linoleum. And there's that bouncy ball the boys have been looking for.*

I was surprised by what I found. I thought I had thoroughly cleaned the kitchen, but on my knees I could see many things I had never seen before.

So it is in my prayer life. Whether I'm literally on my knees or sitting in my big red chair as I usually do when I pray, I'm often amazed to see my perspective change in prayer. First I see the dirt that only God can wash away. Then I discover the treasures Jesus wants to reveal to me in time with Him.

An acronym that has helped me organize my prayer life is the word *ACTS. A* stands for adoration, *C* for confession, *T* for thanksgiving, and *S* for supplication.

Adoration

The greatest treasure you'll discover in your quiet time is God. Look closely at God's Word to find the treasure of who He is. Find a Scripture that illuminates the qualities of God. As you read those verses, your mind will no longer be on you; instead it will be on the Lord of lords and King of kings. Spend some time praising God for who He is and adoring Him. I often read a psalm, such as Psalm 104:1-2: "Bless the LORD, O my soul! O LORD my God, You are very great; You are clothed in splendor and majesty." Let your mind dwell on God's greatness.

Confession

Confession is looking closely enough at your heart to see the dirt in your life. Psalm 139:23-24 is a prayer of confession: "Search me, O God, and know my heart; try me and know my anxious thoughts; and see if there be any hurtful way in me, and lead me in the everlasting way." Sin grieves God. Call sin what it is; it's not a bad habit, a bad choice, or a mistake. Sin is sin, and its roots are rebellion and independence from God. Ask God to reveal to you your sins, and as He does, confess them and ask God to give you strength to turn away from them.

In confession you come to God just as you are with no pretense, no mask. By being honest with God you'll discover a great treasure: He loves you just as you are, and He wants to transform your character to be like His. In confession I remember that all my efforts cannot accomplish this transformation. Only Jesus can.

Thanksgiving

"Give thanks to the LORD, for He is good; for His lovingkindness is everlasting" (Psalm 118:1). Thank God for the big things, for Christ's death and resurrection. Thank God for all He has provided you; thank Him for your husband, your children, your church, and your friends. And when you thank God for these things, be specific. For example, what specific things about your husband can you be thankful for? *Thank You, Lord, that my husband is a hard worker who provides for us, that he is completely trustworthy, that he is a great father to his two sons, and that he loves You, Lord.*

Thank God for the little things that just tickle you and make you smile. Thank Him for the everyday beautiful things, like bright red cardinals, untouched snowfalls, and little boy hugs. A heart overflowing with thanksgiving has no room for complaints and negativity.

Supplication

Supplication entails presenting our requests to God. We can pray about anything and everything! Sometimes we think our desires are not spiritual enough to pray about. We need to remember, however, that God cares about whatever we care about. He wants to hear our honest prayers. We can pray like the psalmist, "Lord, all my desire is before You" (Psalm 38:9).

In Matthew 7:7-8 Jesus tells us to ask: "Ask, and it will be given to you; seek, and you will find; knock, and it will be opened to you. For everyone who asks receives, and he who seeks finds, and to him who knocks it will be opened." Clearly God wants us to ask. Sometimes God will answer our prayers the way we hope, and sometimes He won't. If I've spent time with God, I am more likely to have a heart that lines up with His.

Reading Scripture

Our quiet times will be most effective when we incorporate both prayer and Scripture. Scripture is God's love letter and instruction manual to us. We need to read it daily to see more clearly who we are, whose we are, and how to live as children of God.

We can read Scripture in many ways, and I'll give some suggestions here. The most important thing, however, is just to read God's Word. I have a rule for myself: I do not allow myself to read anything else before I've read His Word. For someone like me who loves to read, that can be a challenge! I see many women today seeking God through secondary sources—sermons, books about God, or Bible studies where we hear others talk about God. Nothing at all is wrong with these activities, but the most important thing we can do to know God is to read His Word. This way we won't just know about God; we'll know God personally. The difference is huge.

Here are some suggestions for your Bible reading:

1. Focus on one book of the Bible at a time instead of jumping around from passage to passage. Use a translation you can understand and an edition with helpful notes.

2. Read Psalms and Proverbs again and again. I've heard that Billy Graham has done this throughout his life. That's a great example!

3. When you study a passage, dig a little deeper by asking
   the following questions:

   • What is the passage about? Put it in your own words.
     What is the primary meaning?

   • What do I learn about God, Jesus, and the Holy
     Spirit?

   • What does it mean to me? How do I apply this pas-
     sage to my everyday living?

4. Try reading through the entire Bible in a year. Many
   Bibles include a yearly reading plan.

5. Above all, open your Bible and read.

Listening to God

Listening to God is a crucial part of our relationship with God. I've
never heard God's audible voice, but I have heard Him speak through
the Holy Spirit's impression on my heart. Sometimes this impression
comes after I've prayed and while I'm being still. Sometimes I hear
God when I'm reading Scripture and a particular truth just leaps off
the pages into my heart—an "aha" moment.

We cannot hear God without the work of the Holy Spirit in our
lives. The Holy Sprit comes to live in us the moment we accept Jesus
as our Lord and Savior. He is a permanent resident in the believer, and
His jobs are numerous: He teaches us and reminds us of Scripture,
convicts of sin, bears fruit in our lives, comforts and helps us, and opens
our eyes to God's truth.

Listening is a crucial part of communication in any relationship.
If we spend all our time with God talking to Him without allowing
Him to speak to us, we are certainly going to miss out on a deeper
relationship with Him.

At first, you might feel uncomfortable or strange sitting still to listen
to God. Your mind might wander all over the place, and you might want
to hop up after less than five minutes of sitting because you've thought
of something you need to do. You'll think of excuses: *I pray all day*

*long, so I really don't need to have a quiet time. I've got so much to do
today; I'll have a quiet time tonight. I don't even know what to do in a
quiet time...*And so the excuses continue.

Press on. Sit down. Keep a notebook by you to jot down distracting
to-do items. Get your Bible, journal, and pen. And just do it! Anything
worth doing takes effort and practice.

Amid the Hustle and Bustle

Once we've had a quiet time, God doesn't want us to go off and
forget Him. He wants us to have ears that hear and eyes that see Him
throughout the day. He'll speak to us in the activities of our everyday
lives—while we're vacuuming, doing laundry, working at a computer,
and carpooling. We need to be sure to be listening.

In *Becoming a Woman Who Listens to God*, author Sharon Jaynes
explains that God is accessible to us all day long, not just during a quiet
time.

> But when I pored over the pages of Scripture, I
> discovered that some of God's most memorable messages
> were not delivered while men and women were away at
> spiritual retreat, but right in the middle of the hustle and
> bustle of everyday life. He spoke to Moses while he was
> tending sheep, to Gideon while he was threshing wheat,
> to Zechariah while he was performing his duties at the
> temple, to shepherds while they were watching their
> flocks by night, to Peter and Andrew while they were
> fishing on the sea, to the woman at the well while she
> was drawing water for her household chores, to Matthew
> while he was busy in his tax office, and to Martha while
> she was baking in the kitchen.[1]

Do You Have a Religion or a Relationship?

We've been discussing how to grow in your walk with Christ, but I
need to back up some. I need to ask: Do you have a relationship with
Christ? God created us to be in a relationship with Him and to know

Him as a child knows his father. "See how a great a love the Father has bestowed on us, that we would be called children of God; and such we are" (1 John 3:1).

My walk with God began when I was a 16-year-old in high school. I kept up a good appearance as a young girl, but deep down inside I knew I was living a lie. I wore a deceptive mask of prettiness, self-confidence, and goodness, but inside all I felt was "not pretty enough," insecure, and rebellious of all authority in my life. When I acknowledged my need for a Savior, I remember not being completely sure what being a Christian meant. But I knew I wanted the peace, love, and assurance Christ promised and other Christians radiated.

What about you? Do you have a relationship with Christ?

God cares personally for you. Luke 12:7 is just one Scripture pointing to God's intimacy with you: "The very hairs of your head are all numbered." He is intimately acquainted with all your ways, and He knew you in your mother's womb. He wants to be in a relationship with you and reveal His plans for you.

God's love for you is real—so real that God's only Son died painfully on a cross so you can have a relationship with Him. When Christ died, He took the punishment of every sin you've ever committed or ever will commit. Nothing can add to or take away from His love for you. He asks you to receive His love, repent of your sins, and turn to Him.

Christ's death and resurrection allow you to be spiritually reborn by His Spirit living in you. As Ephesians 2:4-5 explains, "But God, being rich in mercy, because of His great love with which He loves us, even when we were dead in our transgressions, made us alive together with Christ (by grace you have been saved)." As a Christian you go from death to life, for you have the very life of Christ in you.

In *A Woman's Journey to the Heart of God* Cynthia Heald beautifully describes God's desire for a relationship with us:

> God's invitation is written with the blood of Jesus Christ. When we believe in and accept Christ's atoning sacrifice we are brought into a relationship with our Father that enables us to journey toward His heart of love, forgiveness, reconciliation, and new birth. All God

asks is that we admit our need for a Savior, turn away from the path of sin we have been on, and turn in faith to God with a desire to live for Him.[2]

If you have never asked God to be your Lord and Savior, will you do that now? You can pray this prayer, and right this minute Jesus will become your Savior. As you believe by faith in God's work on the cross, you will be born again (John 3:7), and God's Spirit will come to live in you. You can pray this prayer or use it as a guide to create your own. Just talk to God from your heart with honesty and sincerity.

> Dear Lord, I confess to You that I'm a sinner, and I need Your forgiveness. Thank You for dying on a cross for me so that all my past, present, and future sins will be forgiven. I want to turn away from sin and toward You. Thank You that through Your death and resurrection I can be born again and have a new life. Lord, I believe in You and ask You to show me how to live for You. Amen.

If you prayed this prayer, please tell someone! Find a church home and find Christian women who will help you in your journey with Christ. Begin seeking God by having a quiet time every day.

We've covered a good deal of material in this chapter not specifically about what our husbands need. That's because we as wives must put first things first. We must put our relationship with the Lord first so that we will be prepared and equipped to minister to our husbands.

Time with God will transform us. We'll come to know God better, we'll trust Him more with all areas of our lives, and we'll more readily recognize His voice. As we're focusing on God, we're no longer focusing on our husbands' faults, on the changes we want to happen in our marriages, or on what we feel entitled to as wives. Instead, as we soak in God's love, we become more like Him. We become God's heart of love, hands of love, and eyes of love for our husbands.

Psalm 37:4 reads, "Delight yourself in the LORD; and He will give you the desires of your heart." I can remember a time when I thought this meant God would answer my laundry list of requests. Now, however, I understand that's not at all what this verse is about. It means that as I grow in maturity in my relationship with the Lord, the desires of my heart become more and more like His desires. I have found over the years that knowing the Lord and pleasing Him in my marriage are the desires of my heart. I pray they will be your desires too.

Your Husband's Spiritual Life

God's perfect plan of marriage is for a husband and wife to share intimacy in all ways—emotionally, intellectually, physically, and spiritually. I know many wives who have longed for more spiritual intimacy in marriage. Some husbands are completely open to attending church together, studying the Bible, talking about the Bible, and praying together. Unfortunately many men are not open at all to creating spiritual intimacy.

Earlier in my marriage I had this frustration too. I had been a Christian a long time when Scott and I married, but Scott was a much newer Christian. I made the mistake of pushing and nagging him to be like me spiritually. Now I know God wanted me to pray for my husband. And that's what I did for many years. I stopped the nagging and just prayed for my husband to know God more intimately. Scott is now a man of God and the spiritual leader in our home. I have witnessed how God's power released through prayers will accomplish more in our husbands' lives than nagging, badgering, or manipulating ever will. Trust God to work in your husband's heart to create a desire for spiritual intimacy.

So I want to end this chapter by saying that one of the most loving things you can do for your husband is to pray regularly for him. Remember the commitment statement you signed in the study guide for chapter 1? One part of that is to pray daily for your husband. The most important prayer you can pray for your husband is one I've prayed for myself and my husband for years: that each of us will hunger and thirst for God all the days of our lives.

Let your husband see the fruit of the Spirit in your life: love, joy, and peace. Let him see how you love God's Word. Share with your husband a Scripture verse that's helped you. Live out a life of faith for him to see. Attend church together.

Pray with your husband. If he doesn't want to pray aloud, ask if he'll silently pray with you while you pray aloud. Tell your husband you feel closer to him when you share spiritually.

If your husband is not a believer in Christ, pray for him and love him. Tell God the desire of your heart is for your husband to come to know Christ as his Lord and Savior. Then let God be God in your husband's life. You can be assured that God loves your husband even more than you do.

PRAYER GUIDE

Father God,

Thank You that You created me to know You and to be in a relationship with You. Thank you that I can come to You at any time in prayer and know that You hear me and care for me. Help me to make my relationship with You my number one priority. Father, where I have let other people or activities crowd You out, please forgive me and set me on the right path. I pray that my husband and I will hunger and thirst for You. Help me to entrust my husband to You, knowing that You love him and have a plan for his life. Help us to grow in spiritual intimacy, for I know this will make our marriage stronger and closer. I pray these things in Jesus' name. Amen.

3

What Is a Helper?

One of my main dreams growing up was to get married, have children, and live happily ever after. At the age of 27, living in Atlanta, Georgia and working as a high school English teacher, I'd already celebrated with most of my best friends as they got married. I was beginning to wonder if I'd ever meet my Prince Charming, but then my principal hired a young man from Minnesota to teach math. Scott was (and still is!) cute, friendly, and down-to-earth, and we quickly fell in love.

One year later we were married in my hometown of North Palm Beach, Florida, with hundreds of friends and family in attendance. My fairy-tale wedding day is still one of my happiest memories. I wore a billowy, white Cinderella dress and loved feeling like a princess for a day. My groom was handsome and charming. As we laughed and celebrated on our wedding day, I thanked God for making my dream come true.

The wedding night, however, was not what either of us expected. We arrived at our hotel room with both of us looking forward to the night ahead! Within a few minutes, however, I noticed loud music coming from outside. Looking out the window I saw a band playing an outdoor concert. I knew I could not spend my wedding night with that loud music blaring all night.

"Honey, we cannot stay here. We have to go find another hotel."

Scott looked at me as if I were an alien, but then he calmly replied, "It will be fine. We won't even notice the music after a while."

I was not convinced. I started packing up our bags and announced, "I will not stay here. Either you get the car or I will."

We then proceeded to have one of the biggest fights we'd ever had. I was crying, and we were both screaming.

The night went from bad to worse. We left the hotel in stubborn silence and drove to another hotel about ten minutes away. Unlike the luxurious hotel room we had reserved, this new hotel was budget all the way. The air conditioner was not yet running, so when we got into the room on the night of July 6 in south Florida, the room temperature was close to 100 degrees. I turned on the air conditioner and just lay on the bed in complete misery.

Then, in an attempt to move things toward romance, Scott suggested we use the hot tub in our room. I thought, *Sure—getting hotter than I already am sounds like so much fun.* However, I also wanted to try to save our sabotaged night. I turned on the hot tub and couldn't believe what happened next. The water jets were not pointing down in the tub as they should have been. Instead, they were pointing up, directly toward our bed. The water completely soaked the bed's comforter and sheets.

Finally, all we could do was laugh. No, it was not quite the wedding night we'd expected.

Heavy Suitcases of Expectations

I can assure you that when I first got married, my main thoughts were not about having a godly marriage, one founded on the firm foundation of Christ. I was not thinking about what my husband needed. I was really thinking about what *I* needed and how *I* could live happily ever after. Of course, that meant Scott had a lot to do to make me happy.

Like me, many women enter marriage with a long list of expectations. Couples expect to make each other happy and to find happiness. We expect to enjoy each other's company and to have a lot of time to spend with one another. We expect to love and be loved. We expect our husbands to be attentive, strong, sensitive, smart, godly, romantic, sexy, good, kind, patient, trustworthy, manly, happy, secure, and understanding. And able to leap tall buildings in a single bound!

Then marriage happens. Some of our expectations are met, but many are not. Often we both end up hurt and disappointed. Imagine each of your unrealistic expectations as a suitcase. Here's the suitcase of "make me happy." There's one called "do things my way." Another labeled "be romantic." And on and on. What are your suitcases of expectations labeled?

With these cumbersome suitcases, we stumble along in marriage. The more we try to walk, the more burdensome they become. The joyful trip of marriage that we imagine hasn't even started because we're too worn out from packing!

So what do we do with this load? We lay it down. In one of the sweetest invitations in Scripture, Jesus invites us to find rest in Him. "Come to Me, all who are weary and heavy-laden, and I will give you rest. Take my yoke upon you and learn from Me, for I am gentle and humble in heart, and you will find rest for your souls. For my yoke is easy and my burden is light" (Matthew 11:28-30).

Jesus invites us to lay down our heavy suitcases, the ones making us weary in marriage, and to take up the load He appoints to us. He promises that we can learn from Him what to carry. In addition He offers to be yoked with us. Can you see that picture?

God wants me to carry only the suitcases filled with His expectations of me. He wants my priorities to match His priorities for me. We cannot do everything, and God does not expect us to! We only have time and energy for God's priorities in our lives.

God's Instruction Manual, the Bible

God's Word makes clear that my number one priority is my relationship with God, and my number two priority is my relationship with my husband.

Notice what older women are told to do in Titus 2:4-5: "Encourage the young women to love their husbands, to love their children, to be sensible, pure, workers at home, kind, being subject to their own husbands, so that the word of God will not be dishonored." Notice that loving our husbands comes first in this list of commands, thus showing its importance to God.

What else does God say in the Bible about marriage? To begin with, He says that He created marriage. It was His idea since the beginning of time. He is for marriage in general, and He is for *your* marriage in particular. The first marriage we see in the Bible is the union of Adam and Eve. In Genesis 2 God doesn't even call Eve a wife; instead, God's first label of her is a "helper." This is our starting point for learning what kind of wives God wants us to be.

God's Instructions in Genesis

As we look to God's Word for His direction in marriage, let's start at the beginning. Genesis 2:18 reads, "Then the LORD God said, 'It is not good for the man to be alone; I will make him a helper suitable for him.'" In the verses immediately following we learn that "out of the ground the LORD God formed every beast of the field and every bird of the sky." Adam names all of the creatures and checks all of them out, perhaps looking for a partner, "but for Adam there was not found a helper suitable for him" (Genesis 2:20). So God caused Adam to fall asleep, and from one of Adam's ribs God made Adam's helper, Eve.

Can you imagine Adam's reaction when he wakes and first sees Eve? How his heart must have soared! I imagine them embracing, laughing, and bubbling over with delight. Adam parades Eve around the Garden, proudly displaying her to all the other creatures. He points out his favorite places and creations to her. They become "one flesh" (Genesis 2:24), and they "were both naked and were not ashamed" (Genesis 2:25). They are in complete harmony. Their contentment and satisfaction in being together is at its height. Life is good!

These verses in Genesis provide three guidelines for understanding God's definition of a helper.

First, a helper is a companion.

Second, a helper is suitable to her husband.

Third, a helper is one with her husband.

A Helper Is a Companion

Just like Eve, our first role as wives is to be a companion. God created Eve to be Adam's helper because God called it "not good" for Adam to be alone. God could have decided that it was perfectly good for Adam to be alone, but He didn't. He saw that Adam needed a companion.

A Companion Is a Friend

A helper who is a companion helps meet her husband's need for friendship. In Titus 2:4 we see that wives are to love their husbands, and the love this verse refers to is a brotherly friendship. The dictionary defines *companion* as "a comrade or friend." How is your friendship with your husband? Is it one of your top priorities? Is he your best friend? Women tend to have a handful of friends, but men are more likely to rely on their wives to meet their friendship needs. What a blessing a husband and wife can find in each other's lifelong friendship.

A friend has time to listen to her husband without interrupting or judging. A friend notices her husband has had a long day and doesn't add to his to-do list. She goes to hit golf balls because that's one of his favorite things to do. She savors intimacy with her husband. A friend stops what she's doing to give her husband a hug and a kiss when he walks in the door. A friend plans a fun date with her best friend, her husband.

As I think about Adam and Eve enjoying their togetherness, I have to ask myself how much I'm enjoying my companionship with Scott.

When I was dating Scott, I could not get enough time with him. I remember thinking what a fantastic idea God had that two friends could be married and live together forever! It was just too good to be true! Now, after 15 years of marriage, two children, more responsibilities, and more familiarity with one another, I admit that I often lose sight of the gift of companionship. I so easily let other things crowd out time with my husband. I'm asking God to help me treasure the gift of friendship with my husband.

A Companion Enjoys Togetherness

A helper is a companion who is frequently in the company of another. Of course, this definition of a companion overlaps with the previous one. I love this definition! God wants me to hang out with my husband—how fun! We have many ways to be in each other's company, but we often have to make a conscious effort to choose companionship over what might seem to be urgent tasks. God wants me to set aside my to-do list and my agenda to enjoy my husband.

Simply enjoying little daily pleasures or even doing chores together are ways to increase time together. Pray for God to make you aware of moments to spend with your husband. Here are a few ideas of things to do together: walk the dog, give the kids a bath together, sit side by side at your child's basketball game or dance class, share a bowl of ice cream and conversation while gazing at the stars, hang out with him while he cleans the garage (maybe even help him!), do yard work, or wash the cars. Remember to do these activities together. Dividing responsibilities may be quicker and more efficient, but it may not be more effective. Choose to enjoy your husband's companionship.

Think back to your dating days, a time when you probably had more time to concentrate on one another. What did you like to do while dating? Since we first met, Scott and I have loved watching movies. But we've been so busy lately, especially with our children's activities, that we haven't had much time to hang out together. So the other night, we sent the kids upstairs to bed while we snuggled and watched a movie. We both were refreshed simply by one another's presence.

As this husband's comments reveal, friendship with our husbands is strengthened when we share activities.

> Most married men don't want to abandon their wives to do guy things. They want to do guy things with their wives. They want them to be their playmates. It's no different from when they were dating. For a guy, a big part of the thrill was doing fun things together. The woman who is having fun with her husband is incredibly attractive.

My friend Marybeth and I discussed this idea one day, and not too much later she had an opportunity to apply what she learned.

> My kids and husband were jumping on the trampoline one day, and I decided this was a good chance to join my husband in some play. I ran outside to join them, and I wish you could have heard their delighted shrieks. "Mom's here!" they yelled, and my husband just got the biggest smile on his face. We ended up jumping together for a while—the kids got tired of us and got off. We laughed and laughed as he threatened to bounce me off and almost made me fall down on my wobbly land legs. It was...*fun*. I hardly ever take the time to put down the housework and just have fun—especially with my husband.
>
> As my 13-year-old stood on the porch and looked on (he was too cool to join us), I heard him say, "My parents have completely lost it." But there was no mistaking the huge grin on his face! Yes, that one simple effort on my part certainly made an impression...and hey, jumping on the trampoline is great exercise!
>
> So take my advice and go have fun with your husband. Don't worry if you look foolish—I *know* I did! And yet my actions spoke volumes of love to him, and etched a memory in our hearts and the hearts of our children forever.

After Marybeth told me this story, I was inspired and motivated to join my husband in some fun too. But I have to say what really made a lasting impression on me was her husband Curt's rendition of this simple moment.

> Something magical happened today. After mowing the grass, I started jumping on the trampoline. And of course my two younger boys had to come out and make fun of how silly I looked. While we were joking back and forth, suddenly my wife appeared with a huge grin on her face. She was going to get on.
>
> "I haven't done this since I was a kid," she laughed as she started bouncing. Her legs were wobbly, and she was trying to keep upright, and her smile got bigger. And as she jumped higher, she started to laugh. And I don't mean "laugh" like heard-a-cute-joke laugh. Suddenly my 35-year-old wife was laughing like a little kid. I hadn't heard that sound from her in longer than I can remember. It was so beautiful that my heart began to hurt. She and I were jumping and laughing together as if we had stepped back in time to a day when life was more childlike and innocent and fun.
>
> Why do couples get caught up with so many responsibilities and forget that they can have fun and laugh together? She and I have been guilty of that. But I remembered on the trampoline why I fell in love with my wife. We were young and had fun and laughed together. She was my best friend, and I wanted to spend the rest of my life with her. I wanted to open up my heart to her and give her every part of me. Life has been hard, and we've been struggling lately. But I decided that I'm going to make sure that we remember that we can laugh.

What can you do to build fun and relaxing together times into your marriage? Here are a few ideas: Go downtown and be a tourist, try a new restaurant, go out to breakfast, take a class together, cook together, play a board game, attend a professional sports event, visit a museum, go to a play, go bowling, play laser tag, ride bikes, go for a hike, drive through the country and stop for a picnic, play tennis or golf, sing and dance at a concert, and join your husband in whatever activity he likes! If you can arrange it, go away for a night or two together. As you make time for fun and laughter, you're strengthening the foundation of friendship in your marriage.

Togetherness helps diffuse arguments that arise simply because you haven't enjoyed each other's company frequently enough. Another benefit of togetherness is that it prepares your marriage for tough times ahead. While you spend your lives together, whether it's doing ordinary daily chores or making time for fun, you're cementing the bond in your marriage. It's a bond that will need to be strong when stormy weather prevails.

A Companion Completes Her Husband

Last, a companion is "one of a pair or set of things; a mate." This definition implies the idea of two things that are incomplete without the other. For some reason I couldn't help thinking of trying to find missing socks! No, wives are not missing socks, but as husbands and wives we go together. We are life-mates. We complement one another as we share life's journeys.

For examples, our boys know they can wrestle, play ball, and talk to their dad about anything, but they also know that Scott means business when it comes to discipline. I am so thankful for his voice of authority in our family. I complement him by bringing a female's tenderness to parenting while I follow through with the guidelines he's established. When a husband and wife are united in purpose, their relationship becomes a partnership. They complete each other.

Michelle is a friend who complements her husband. She shares how her role as a helper has changed along with the seasons of her marriage.

> After the birth of our three children our marriage clearly took on a new form. With my husband traveling up to five days each week, I found myself living the life of a single mom during the week, only to face what we referred to as "reentry" on the weekends. When I finally came to the realization that this situation was not going to change anytime soon, I decided I better change my response to it.

Another turning point for my marriage occurred around this same time when in the midst of a heated discussion my husband reminded me that he was not responsible for my happiness! And he was right. I made some deliberate choices to set myself up to better enjoy long weeks without him. We joined a large local church that offered many services, Bible studies, children's ministries, and activities.

The real balancing act became evident on the weekends themselves. My husband came home exhausted and depleted after a long week of travel and hotel living. He needed to be replenished and restored. And I needed time alone with him as well as help with the children and the household. I learned to help him make the most of his time at home and tried to give him time for rest and recreation with friends just for fun! In this season of our marriage, I learned what unconditional love was. I could not possibly meet my family's needs without strength from the Lord. Being my husband's helper required me to meet my family's needs and let Jesus meet mine.

As the children grew and we faced the new challenge of raising teenagers, our relationship once again transformed. We clearly needed to be unified in our family struggles. By recognizing this early on, we found that these were the years that forged a love and commitment to each other that we had not yet experienced! Communication became our utmost priority. Prayer became our most valuable resource. The sheer vulnerability of this stage of our shared lives made us recognize even more our total dependence on God for strength.

Our nest is now empty, and our relationship can once again take priority. Our love has come full circle, and we find in each other the friendship that drew us together at first. We have discovered a true partnership as we seek to enjoy the second half of our lives together. Our shared experiences have left us with a fresh perspective that life is short and without guarantees. Also, we recognize that what really matters most is the love that we share with each other, family, and friends. Our shared passion for ministry is at the center of all that we do. Our commitment to Christ is our joy and strength.

A Helper Is Suitable to Her Husband

Genesis 2 reveals a second aspect of being a helper: A wife is to be suitable to her own husband. First, I need to help! A helper serves her husband. I become suitable to my husband by praying for God to show me how to help my husband, observing what is helpful to him, and asking him what he needs help with. Then I need to make sure I do whatever God reveals.

I need to make helping my husband a top priority before I help anyone else. Sometimes women can spend so much time helping children, friends, relatives, and church ministries that by the time they get to their husbands, they have nothing left to give.

I read Elizabeth George's book *A Woman After God's Own Heart* as a young Christian, and its principles have lived with me many years. Here is one of the principles I've remembered: Don't give away to others what you have not first given away at home. She explains that this practice came to her one day after she had spent many hours making a splendid meal for a woman in her church who had just had a baby. Her two little girls wanted to know who the meal was for, so Elizabeth told them, taking advantage of a good opportunity to teach her girls about giving. Then they asked…

> "What are we having for dinner?" When I said that we were having macaroni and cheese with hot dogs (again!), I was sharply convicted of my wrong priorities. I had put someone else…ahead of my own family. I had gone *many* extra miles to make the meal I was taking to someone I had never met but I was throwing together something quick and easy for my own husband and children. In short, I was giving something to someone else that I had not first given to the people closest to me![2]

God wants me to make helping my husband a top priority, and God wants me to be specifically suited to *my* husband, not anyone else's. A woman I knew many years ago put much effort into making gourmet meals for her husband. Finally, her husband gently told her that he really just wanted a meal he could eat in one bowl, like a casserole!

Another way to be a helper for my husband is to help him do what God has instructed him to do. In Ephesians 5:23,25 we find one of the guidelines for husbands: "For the husband is the head of the wife, as Christ also is the head of the church…Husbands, love your wives, just as Christ also loved the church and gave Himself up for her." Also, in addition to leading our family and loving me, my husband is to provide for and protect his family.

Mike explains how his wife, Amy, helps him to go out and do his job of being a pilot:

> Amy makes me feel loved by always trying to do little things for me. The little things may seem trivial, but they make the most difference. She irons my clothes for work, makes a sandwich before I leave, and has something to eat when I walk in at night. When she does little things in a nice way, the bigger issues are easier to work through. Her constant love makes me want to show her the same amount of love in return, although I never will be able to!

How are you doing at supporting your husband's role of leader, provider, and protector? Unfortunately, I can remember way too many times when I tried to usurp his role, especially his leadership role. Scott and I can laugh about one particular incident now, but at the time, nothing was funny about it.

When we first moved to Charlotte for my husband's new job with US Airways, we lived in an apartment until we could determine where to settle more permanently. For many months Scott searched the Internet for homes and areas to raise our family. We piled the family in the car countless times to drive around looking at homes.

One day we drove a considerable distance from our apartment. As we drove I kept telling Scott I didn't want to live so far out. He kept saying just to have an open mind, that he'd done lots of research and knew we could get more house for our money in Union County, which was on the outskirts of Charlotte. What's more, the schools were great, an important consideration for us with two little boys.

I continued to voice my skepticism until finally Scott pulled the car over, turned around, and drove back to the apartment. We never even saw the houses he wanted to look at that day.

Ouch! Retelling this story hurts! But it's a reminder to me and hopefully to you to let our husbands play the role God planned for them. The end of the story is that we bought a beautiful house about a mile from the very place we turned around. My husband knew what he was talking about. I really can trust him to lead.

We need to remember that husbands and wives have different roles that are equally valued and needed. Sometimes wives mistakenly think that God's instruction for them will turn them into doormats who let their husbands take advantage of them.

You can trust God in the role He's assigned you. Let Him direct your steps in the path He wants you to take. He promises to be your Teacher and to show you one step at a time how to do what He commands. With each step He'll transform you into the wife He wants you to be and your husband needs you to be.

Some of the negativity about our roles undoubtedly comes from a misunderstanding of what roles are. Our role is just that, a role; it's not our identity. My identity is based on who I am and to whom I belong. My identity is this: I am a child of God (1 John 3:1), I am a new creature in Christ (2 Corinthians 5:17), and I am no longer a slave to sin (Romans 6:6). God's Word determines your identity; your actions don't, and neither do your roles. Knowing who you are frees you to be you. God created you, and He will use your uniqueness to complement your husband's.

Being Your Husband's Helper—Even When He's Away

Many women today are married to husbands whose jobs require them to travel, and this situation carries its own particular challenges.

My husband has been a pilot for most of our marriage, so I know firsthand some of the trials of having a traveling husband. You're left to hold down the fort on your own. The responsibilities of running a home, perhaps working yourself, and tending to the kids all fall on your shoulders. You're forced to be fairly independent while he's away, but then you need to suddenly become a team player again when your husband returns.

Elizabeth's marriage to Brian has always included being a helper to her traveling husband. Brian was a Marine pilot when they married, and now he's an airline pilot. Elizabeth truly ministers to her husband by adapting her life to his needs. He knows that he is a priority to her even when he's not at home. She shares two practices—positive phone calls and a homecoming ritual—that she uses to serve her husband.

> When Brian was able to phone occasionally, I learned to take the opportunity to encourage him with lighthearted stories of home and hearth and let him talk with his babies as I cradled the phone on their shoulders. Tales of toddler escapades took precedent over the saga of the broken dryer, trips to the pediatrician, and unexpected bills. Ending the conversation on a high note was important because these connections were few and far between. Even now, when technology allows us to talk more frequently, I continue to use these check-ins to produce an air of comfort and anticipation of our reunion.
>
> To some this system may sound a bit contrived, as if I put on a happy face while secretly hiding the not-so-happy stuff. But wives who are often on their own while their husbands are away are wise to develop a system for handling everyday problems. At the same time, we have to establish criteria to know when sharing the burden is beneficial. Communicating every dirty little detail that went wrong with your day does little to buoy your husband's spirits after a long day away from the familiar. I do have the burden of being both parents to our children and running a household, but I still get to enjoy being home. My husband, however, has the burden of his work, plus the discomfort of being away from home and family. Worrying about his wife's burden as well as his own will wear down even the most optimistic husband. It will divide his attention between duty and home, diminishing his effectiveness to do either. Only resentment and frustration can result.
>
> For example, if something fails (and it always does) or one of the kids has a problem, I detemine whether my husband would benefit in any way by knowing about it while he is away. If the problem is an emergency, by all means, get your husband involved.

When our middle son fell while in-line skating and suffered a serious compound fracture, I knew my husband would want to know and perhaps find a way to fly home. But instead of calling him immediately to tell him the news, I waited to inform him until I had seen the whole picture, conversed with the doctors, learned of the necessary surgery, and prepared myself to calmly present the entire situation to my husband. My level assessment of the details lessened the panic Brian might feel being told this type of news while away. Brian and I prayed through the surgery, and he was at Collin's bedside early the following morning.

In addition to keeping phone calls positive, I've learned that the homecoming is one of the hidden blessings for the wife of an often-absent husband. The anticipation of togetherness after a separation keeps a marriage young and vibrant. Use it to your full advantage. Whether your husband has been away a day or a month, plan something special for his return. This doesn't have to be extravagant! It can something as simple as a commitment to meet him at the door with a smile and a *real* kiss. Or prepare a simple plate of appealing food and light a candle. Whatever you do, create a warm and inviting environment for him to come home to. This ritual is a way to thank your hardworking spouse for providing for you and your family.

When my husband returns home, our boys vie for his attention. They too have stories to tell, adventures to share. I love watching this contest, and how my husband deftly divides his time between them. But they know that once they have had their time, Mom and Dad need *their* time. We then adjourn to a comfortable, quiet place and spend time catching up on the time while we were separated. This ritual has blessed us both with more peace and stability within our marriage and family life.

Over the years of our friendship, I've admired the way Elizabeth embraces her role as a helper to her husband. I can't help but think that God knew Elizabeth and Brian were perfectly suited to one another.

A Wife Is One with Her Husband

The third and final aspect of being a helper is oneness or intimacy. Let's look at Genesis once again. "For this reason a man shall leave his father and his mother, and be joined to his wife; and they shall become one flesh. And the man and his wife were both naked and were not ashamed" (Genesis 2:24).

Physical intimacy helps to create oneness. God created sexual intimacy as an expression of a husband's and wife's love and commitment to each other. Wives need to remember that for most men, sex is a top priority! Since we're talking about being a husband's helper, we can say that sex helps your husband! For men, sex is the door that opens their hearts to closeness emotionally, mentally, and spiritually.

Oneness comes also through a relationship that is open emotionally, intellectually, spiritually, and physically. God says that in marriage we'll be even closer than close; we'll become one. In Mark 10:8-9 Jesus repeats the words in Genesis: "And the two shall become one flesh; so they are no longer two, but one flesh. What therefore God has joined together, let no man separate." Oneness thrives in a relationship that is permanent and committed to lasting faithfulness. A marriage that reflects this oneness is like a new identity. Two individuals have become something more; they have added a sense of "us" and "we." Scott needs me to act on what is best for us, not just what is best for me.

The minute we get married we are one. We develop the unique qualities of our oneness through the years of marriage. "A marriage is not a joining of two worlds, but an abandoning of two worlds in order that one new one might be formed."[3] What seemed more natural to me when I first married was to be two unique individuals. And certainly Scripture confirms that God values our uniqueness.

However, in creating marriage God put His stamp of approval on something beyond individuality. God's gold star in marriage goes to oneness and unity. The longer I'm married, the more I see that I don't need to fear losing my identity as I obey God's commands for marriage. No, just the opposite, in fact. I find that in marriage I have become more *me*, more the woman God created me to be. I think that's always the case in obeying God: We become our true selves.

Over the years I've learned that oneness in marriage must be guarded and cultivated. My own parents have been a beautiful example of this. They've been married more than 40 years. They both have busy and fruitful lives individually, but they've been committed to finding common ground to knit them together. For example, they have hiked together for years and have enjoyed numerous cross-country hikes in England, combining their mutual love for travel, fitness, and adventure. They are also gracious and generous hosts who love to cook and entertain. They've welcomed countless guests into their home, making each feel loved and embraced. My parents' mutual interests help them enjoy their oneness.

How might you increase the sense of oneness in your marriage? Without being purposeful about oneness, we can so easily allow independence and isolation to worm its way into marriage, slowly loosening the threads that weave us together.

Spiritual Warfare

God's design is for a wife to be a helper who is a companion perfectly suited to her husband, sharing a bond that is closer than any other human relationship. However, I know my marriage doesn't always reflect this design. One of the reasons is that Satan seeks to destroy marriage.

Let's return to Adam and Eve in the Garden of Eden. As Adam is giving Eve the tour of the Garden, they stop before the tree of knowledge of good and evil. Adam explains the instructions God gave him: They can eat from any of the other trees, but not from this one or they will die. My heart aches as I picture them standing there so innocently, hand in hand. In their complete bliss they have no idea that this very spot will be the place of their downfall.

In Genesis 3, the serpent, described as "more crafty than any beast," tempts Eve by questioning God's commands. When Eve responds, she repeats God's command incorrectly. She says that "from the fruit of the tree which is in the middle of the garden, God has said, 'You shall not eat from it or touch it, or you will die.'" What God had really commanded is that they not eat from the tree. He said nothing about touching it. Eve distorts God's Word. God gives us His commands for our good and our protection. The truth of this is vividly revealed in what transpires in the Garden of Eden.

Eve could have stopped the serpent right then and there, but instead she listens to him. Sensing his receptive audience, Satan goes on to tempt Eve by promising her knowledge that will make her like God. Eve takes the bait, bites the delightful and desirable fruit, and furthers her offense by offering the fruit to Adam. He takes a bite, their eyes are opened, and they hide from God. God punishes Adam and Eve, banning them from the Garden. How utterly heartbreaking.

Satan attacked the very first marriage, and marriage continues to be a battlefront. Satan will try to make you think that your husband is the enemy, but the true enemy is Satan. As we respond to God in obedience by being helpers, Satan will intensify the battle. Satan is a tempter, a deceiver, and a liar, and he uses his tools against you in your marriage. However, that's all he is. Because of Jesus Christ's death and resurrection, Satan does not have power over us. Satan may engage us in battle, but Christ has ultimately won. This is not a battle even to think of fighting on our own. We will need Christ's power and our spiritual armor (Ephesians 6:10-18).

As I'm writing this book I've had so many opportunities to practice the principles in it. Yesterday before church I let one little thing Scott said to me become a huge issue. I had to leave early for church to serve in children's ministry. Consequently, Scott would get the kids fed, dressed, and out the door with him to church. Scott is very much a partner in all matters concerning our children, so normally this would have been no big deal to him. This particular morning, however, Scott responded to me with frustration, saying I needed to take the kids with me. Well, of course, I had to be at church immediately and had no time to alter my plans.

Satan's lies were loud: *You're only asking him to help this one time. He doesn't understand or appreciate all you do. He's just thinking of himself.* I chose to listen to the lies, and they became fuel for my irritation and hurt feelings.

Scott knew something was bothering me. He asked me what it was, and I told him. However, before that I had prayed. I felt free to tell him what I was feeling because I had asked God to help us reach an understanding. My prayer went something like this: *God, I am so mad at what Scott said this morning, and I think he was just plain wrong. I don't like feeling this way, so please help us to talk and move past this. Help me to have a soft heart toward him. Help me to try to see things from his perspective and Your perspective, Lord.*

The Holy Spirit softened my heart. When we talked, I truly tried to see Scott's point of view. I realized that Scott wasn't purposefully being unhelpful; he was just overwhelmed with all he had to do.

I also realized that my response was based on fear—a fear of not being appreciated. Can you identify any fears keeping you from being your husband's helper? Satan will use our fears as footholds into the sacred ground of marriage. I can slam the door on Satan by taking up the armor of God and reminding myself of the truth. I can refuse Satan's lies by calling on Jesus.

A Wife Is Not the Holy Spirit

A word of caution: Being your husband's helper does not open the door for you to give advice, suggest, manipulate, nag, direct, fix, or in any way to try to change him. Unfortunately, we women try so often to be our husbands' Holy Spirit. Many men I have talked with commented on their distaste for wives who try to change them. "Being a helper does not mean she should tell me what to do all the time," explains Phillip. Tony said, "Do not confuse *helper* with *director* or *critic.*"

Get out of God's way and let God change your husband. "In the same way, you wives, be submissive to your own husbands so that even if any of them are disobedient to the word, they may be won without a word by the behavior of their wives" (1 Peter 3:1). Did you notice how a wife can influence her unbelieving or disobedient husband? Without a word! By her behavior!

As wives, our first job assignment is to be helpers to our husbands. Being a helper means being my husband's friend, serving him, and developing closeness with him. Only as I look at my role through God's eyes can I embrace this job assignment from God. My friend Amy wrote in an e-mail, "I think when God made me a wife, He gave me a very special and honored title." What a sweet and right perspective she has of being a wife. May you and I have the same perspective as we treasure our role as helpers to our husbands.

PRAYER GUIDE

Dear Lord,

Just as You breathed life into Adam, I pray You will breathe life into my marriage. Show me any expectations, hurts, or fears that might be weighing down my marriage so that I can confess them and move on. Thank You for the gift of my husband. Thank You that I'm not alone in life, that You've given me a life partner. Show me ways to be his friend, lover, and helper. Show me ways to communicate in my words and actions that he's my top priority. I want to help him, not hinder him in his role as a husband. Lord, I trust You and Your commands for my marriage. I pray in the name of Jesus. Amen.

4

A Heart of Love

~⚬~

Scott and I were walking down the hallway in the school where we both taught when he suddenly stopped, put his hand on his chest, and said, "My heart just did something funny."

Concerned, I asked him if he was sick and if he had seen a doctor.

He smiled as he explained, "No, I know what's wrong with me."

"You do?" I questioned.

"Yes, I'm lovesick."

That may have been a little corny, but it was also romantic! When he said that to me 16 years ago, he became assured of a little more of my heart.

I love to reminisce about our dating, engagement, and wedding days. Those were the days when romance was at its height. Not to say that we haven't included romance along the way! But other expressions of our love have been more prominent in some seasons of our marriage. One of the treasures of marriage is that in this unique relationship we are allowed full expression of love in all forms. In this chapter we'll look at three forms of love that husbands need from their wives: romantic love, sexual love, and unconditional love.

A Husband Needs His Wife to Love Him Romantically

If you haven't thought about your courtship days in a while, take some time to think about them now. When we were dating, Scott and I just couldn't see one another or talk to one another enough. We worked at the same high school, so we would try to catch glimpses of one another during the day. I would frequently stop at a convenience store on the way to work to buy him his favorite morning drink, a huge Diet Coke. During the day I might ask a student to deliver a note to him. After school, we'd recap the day and then make plans to see one another later. We'd have a date at night, often dinner or a movie, say our goodbyes, and then end the night by talking—again—on the phone!

God created romantic love. Just check out the book of love in the Bible, Song of Solomon. This book is a beautiful allegory of God's love for His people, the church. But we must not forget it's also a true-life love story.

" 'How beautiful you are, my darling, how beautiful you are! Your eyes are like doves.' 'How handsome you are my beloved, and so pleasant!' " (Song of Solomon 1:15-16). Reading this book will convince any doubters that God created romantic love for us to enjoy.

Marriage requires the glue of many forms of love, including romantic love. Romantic love causes us to delight in one another and to be excited by one another. It keeps alive the adventure of being pursued and chosen by another. Romantic love lifts our love beyond the routine and ordinary and can provide an emotional connection.

Keeping Romance Alive

If you've been married very long, you know how easily romantic love can fall by the wayside. Perhaps you're having some pretty dismal thoughts about the chances of romantic love being a part of your relationship. Maybe you're recalling forgotten anniversaries or unromantic birthday presents, such as a new blender. Maybe you're thinking your husband is willing to be romantic only if it leads to sex. We'll discuss that next, but for now open your mind and your heart!

Instead of waiting for your husband to be romantic, go ahead and try initiating romance yourself. That's right—you! Sometimes we women cling to the silly notion that spelling it out for our husbands ruins the romance. We want our husbands to read our minds and create the romantic evening we've always dreamed of. Well, frankly, we need to get over it! If we don't invest in romantic love, we take the risk that our marriage will become dull, boring, and disconnected. More marriages die because two people drift apart than because of a crisis, such as infidelity.

Also, many women believe a myth that I think Satan really gets a kick out of. I think we've bought Satan's lie that men are not romantic. Most men, however, want romance in their marriages. Shaunti Feldhahn's survey in *For Women Only* offers proof. When she asked, "Regardless of whether you are able to plan romantic events, or whether your wife/ significant other appreciates it, do you, yourself desire romance? 84% of the men responded yes, very much or yes, somewhat."[1]

Maybe your husband's idea of romance looks a little different from yours. Maybe he's deathly afraid of being vulnerable and looking like a fool by being romantic. Maybe you'll have to build up his confidence and be creative to resurrect romantic love, but the results will be worth the effort!

Romantic love is the type of love that fills relationships with intrigue, mystery, passion, and energy. It's that intangible quality that initially draws us to one another, causes us to fall in love, and can help us stay in love. As you grow in marriage, the way you express romance may change too, but you need to make sure it's always present in your marriage.

When you're thinking of ways to romance your husband, try to be creative, surprising, and adventuresome. Try to think of what's romantic to your husband. Try some things you did in the old days. You can even ask your husband to give you some ideas!

Ideas for Romantic Love

- Plan a date from start to finish, making all the arrangements.

- Ask him questions as if you were on a date: Where would you like to go on vacation someday? If you had four hours to spend doing whatever you want, what would you do?

- Look him deep in the eyes and listen intently.

- Watch your wedding video.

- Go to the place where you first kissed, had your first date, or got engaged, and tell him you'd choose him again.

- Leave him notes in surprising places—his car, his briefcase, or his suitcase.

- Write him a letter telling him all the reasons you think he's sexy.

- Flirt with him.

- Look beautiful for him.

- Greet him with candles lit and his favorite song playing.

- Call him just to say "I love you."

A Husband Needs His Wife to Love Him Sexually

My 11-year-old son loves sports, so he regularly tunes into ESPN. The other night I watched with him and was shocked by the sexual commercials. To say we live in a sex-saturated culture is an understatement. We can't help but be soaked in mistaken and distorted views about sex from the world. So let's take some time to consider God's perspective on sex.

God created sex as a gift to a married couple to be enjoyed exclusively in marriage. Let's look again at Song of Solomon, a book where a couple delights in romance and sex. "I am my beloved's, and his desire is for me. Come, my beloved, let us go out into the country, let us spend the night in the villages. Let us rise early and go to the vineyards; let us see…whether the pomegranates have bloomed. There I will give you my love" (Song of Solomon 7:10-12). Let's remember God wants us to enjoy sex, be passionate with our husbands, and like the woman in the Song of Solomon, offer our love to our husbands through sex.

God gave us the gift of sex not only for our pleasure but also that we may become one flesh. Let's return to Adam and Eve in the Garden of Eden. "For this reason a man shall leave his father and his mother, and be joined to his wife; and they shall become one flesh. And the man and his wife were both naked and were not ashamed" (Genesis 2:24-25). Sex is not just a physical act; it's a spiritual act too. Something supernatural happens in sex—we become one with our husbands.

I love the last part of these verses in Genesis. Adam and Eve are naked but not ashamed. God's design for oneness includes a spiritual, emotional, intellectual, and physical element. We are given sex as a gift to reveal to one another all that we are, to become physically naked and emotionally naked. And we can take this risk because of the fidelity and security of a permanent marriage commitment. We can be vulnerable without fear, without being ashamed. Sex alone will not create oneness, but it both expresses and celebrates intimacy in marriage.

When we get right down to it, we rarely think about all the things God intended sex to mean. That's why we're taking the time to think about God's perspective right now. Sexual love is a glue that is designed just for marriage with incredibly strong, supernatural, bonding power!

Light His Fire

When we enjoy sex, we are offering our husbands one of the greatest gifts we can give. Okay, Scott only half-jokingly says it's the best gift in the world! But he tells me that he enjoys sex more when he knows I'm enjoying it too. When he knows physical intimacy is important to me, not just to him, he feels loved.

My friend Katherine is a very busy woman with four sons and a decorating business of her own. Despite the many people and activities filling her life, she stepped out of her comfort zone to extend love to her husband.

Pete and I have been married 15 wonderful years. He has been God's perfect gift for me, and I know beyond any shadow of a doubt that God handpicked him for me. Ever since we were married, though, Peter has wanted glamorous photos of me (I did *not* say naked!). But because I've never been ecstatic about the way I look, I kept putting him off and not taking his request seriously. He never pressured me to go to the photo shops in the mall because he knew they made me uncomfortable. But he would gently remind me that he loves me, *all* of me, and that he loves the way I look even if I don't.

So when I became good friends with a photographer, an idea came to mind. I decided to do a photo shoot right before our 15-year wedding anniversary.

My friend and I had a lot of giggles and a lot of fun trying to be as sexy as possible without being too revealing! What a hoot! Anyway, when I gave the pictures to Pete on our anniversary, he was overcome with emotion. He was shocked and thrilled that I would do something like that for him after 15 years. He knew how uncomfortable I must have been, which I was, but he quickly realized how much I must love him to do that for him. He appreciated and accepted the pictures for what they were—my true love gift!

We can ask God to help us be more sexually minded. This way we'll be more intentional about making sex a priority. Here are some ideas to get you started.

Ideas for Loving Sexually

- Create a trail of clothes leading to you.
- Write with lipstick a tantalizing message on your bathroom mirror.
- Kiss and hug a lot.
- Enjoy sex at different times of the day.
- Surprise him by waking him up in the middle of the night to make love.
- Don't go very long without making love.

- Massage him from head to toe.

- Do something ordinary, like cook dinner, in sexy lingerie (minus the kids of course!)

- Call him and use a sexy voice to tell him you have a surprise for him when he gets home.

- Be wild and crazy and passionate.

- Drop hints during the day to let him know you're thinking about sex.

- Sleep naked.

- Go away from home, kids, and responsibilities. Get a hotel room for a weekend. Surprise him by making all the arrangements.

- Pray for God to give you freedom in expressing your sexuality.

A Husband Needs His Wife to Love Him Unconditionally

Scott had just gotten his first commercial airline job and had moved from Atlanta to Florida. One-year-old Zachary and I stayed behind in Atlanta so I could finish my year of teaching. We would follow Scott to Florida in June when the school year ended.

We sold our house, so Zachary and I lived in an apartment for a couple of months. This apartment building was six stories high, and it had a garbage chute. Instead of lugging full garbage bags downstairs, all I had to do was toss the bags in the chute. I loved this perk, for getting out the door with a one-year-old and his necessary supplies for the day was cumbersome enough without adding garbage bags to the load.

Being apart from one another was stressful, but we both thought I should keep my commitment to my teaching job till the end of the school year. Scott visited us as often as he could.

One weekend when he came for a visit, he was looking forward to getting the sizeable tax refund check we had just received. His plan was to deposit it in the new checking account in Florida. As he packed his suitcase to return to his job for the week, he couldn't find the refund check. We searched high and low for a long time.

Finally, Scott realized what had happened. He knew that this was a stressful time for us, and he also knew I get a little quirky when I'm stressed. I throw things away. That's right. I feel less stressed when I go through stuff and purge!

Scott knew I had probably had a little throwing-away session. He gently asked me if by chance I thought I might have accidentally thrown away the refund check.

I assured him I couldn't have possibly done that; it was quite a bit of money, and I knew how much we needed it for moving expenses. I had been very careful with it, and I was sure it would turn up.

The check did not turn up, and Scott became more and more convinced I had thrown away the check. He calmly told me he was going to the "garbage room," where all the chutes emptied out. He was going to go through the garbage bags and try to find that check.

Just the thought of this made me cry. I did not want my husband to wade through stinky garbage! However, in the back of my mind I knew he might be right about the check being in the garbage. So off he went while I continued to turn the apartment upside down, searching for the check. All the while I was praying that I had not thrown that check away!

About two hours later, in walked Scott with a terrible smell, a triumphant look on his face, and the check in his hand. He explained that the whole two hours he had opened and dumped out garbage bags. He was on the verge of giving up, but he said one last prayer. When he looked up he saw a garbage bag stuck in the chute. He pulled it out, opened it up, and realized he'd found our garbage bag. And sure enough, in that bag was our tax refund check.

We love remembering this miracle. But to me the greater miracle was the way Scott handled the situation. He never got mad at me, and he never said "I told you so!" Almost ten years later, I remember this as one of the times I felt most loved by my husband.

Scott showed me God's love, a love that sees the faults but doesn't focus on them. This unconditional love is the kind of love our husbands need from us.

Love in Action

Marriage gives me a unique perspective of my husband. I know him better than anyone else in the world, and that's the way God planned it. The unique intimacy that my husband and I share in marriage is one of my greatest blessings—and one of life's greatest challenges! If I'm not careful, my feelings of love can bounce all over the place. One minute I can think my husband is "it on a stick," but the next minute I can be fuming as I think to myself, *You can fly a 737, but you can't put your dirty clothes in the hamper!*

God's commandment to love is not a feeling; rather, it's a call to action. Christians are told in Colossians 3:14 to "put on love." Just as we choose the outfit that will clothe us each day, we also can choose the attitude of love to clothe us. Any wife will admit that more times than she can count, she doesn't feel like showing love to her husband. In those times, rather than putting on love, we'd like to put on irritation, anger, and bitterness. That's exactly when God wants us to recognize that He has poured His love into us so we can pour out His love to our husbands.

Paul defines a specific kind of love—*agape* love, best translated as unconditional love—in 1 Corinthians 13:4-8:

> Love is patient, love is kind and is not jealous; love does not brag and is not arrogant, does not act unbecomingly; it does not seek its own, is not provoked, does not take into account a wrong suffered, does not rejoice in unrighteousness, but rejoices with the truth; bears all things, believes all things, hopes all things, endures all things. Love never fails.

These verses show us the kind of love God has for us, and it's the same kind of love God wants us to show our husbands. As I read these characteristics of God's love, I know that many times I haven't loved my husband this way. I can read this list and also wonder how I will ever love Scott this way. Authors Chuck and Nancy Missler provide a clear explanation of God's agape love.

Agape is not a natural love, but a "supernatural" Love.
We can't produce this kind of Love in our own strength
and ability. To love with God's Love is a matter of our will:
it's a volitional choice. It's not: "I will love this person if
its kills me" (with human love it probably will). But it's:
"I choose to set my self (all my thoughts, emotions and
desires that are contrary to God's) aside and allow God
to love this person through me. I willingly give God my
life to do this."[2]

To love our husbands with God's love, we choose to empty ourselves
of negative thoughts or feelings about our husbands. We choose to bring
this negativity to God and leave it with Him. If we've in any way held
on to anger, bitterness, hurt, or resentment toward our husbands and
then acted on this negativity, we confess this as sin. Then we are free
to love our husbands supernaturally.

I know that for much of my marriage I've loved Scott based on
conditions—I love you if you make me happy, if you serve me, if you
do things the way I hope you will. So learning to let go of my self-will
is an ongoing process of examining myself before the Lord, confessing
sin, and then bearing fruit, one of which is loving my husband.

As a Christian I know from Romans 8:38-39 that nothing "will be
able to separate us from the love of God, which is in Christ Jesus." Sin
doesn't cause God to remove His love from us, but sin does block God's
love flowing through us. Sin is like a rock stopping the flow of water
through a pipe. The water is there but can't get where it's supposed
to go. Remove the rock and the water can flow. Confessing sin and
sincerely repenting leads to God's agape love flowing freely. Living
with God's love flowing through us will gradually replace our old way
of living based on conditional love.

Read 1 Corinthians 13:4-8 again, replacing the word *love* with the
word *God*. Then read through the verses again, replacing the word
love with your own name: Melanie is patient, Melanie is kind…Next,
replace the word *love* with your husband's name: Scott is patient, Scott
is not jealous, Scott does not brag…As you read these verses this way,

make them a prayer for you and your husband. God's love is an action, not a feeling.

The most distinguishing mark of God's love is sacrifice. While on earth, Jesus modeled sacrificial love.

> Christ crushes the myth that love is based upon thinking nice thoughts or feeling gushy emotions. He pushes the definition of love to a higher level—where behavior and belief combine into godly action. Love is no longer a schoolyard romance or a relationship dictated by compatibility; rather, real love is and has always been, a mother stumbling to her baby's bed for the fifth time in one night, or a passenger giving up his place in a lifeboat to save someone else from a sinking ship. Love is Christ on a cross, dying for us, even while we were still lost in our sin (Romans 5:8).[3]

Do you sacrifice for your husband? In little things and big, do you put his interests, desires, and preferences before your own? When you love sacrificially you run an errand that he would normally do, you wash his car for him, you plan a date, you stay home with him instead of going out with girlfriends, you stay up to see him when he comes home late from work, or you follow your husband's leading to a better job in a new city. Loving sacrificially means you want what is best for your husband and your marriage more than you want what is best for you personally.

Our Father's Heart

Over the years I've heard a variety of people make remarks about how my sons remind them of Scott or of me. Zachary is like his father in that he's a leader and he loves sports, but he's like me in his quietness. Tyler reminds people of Scott because of his impish smile and his talkative personality. I love to hear these comments. It's a sign that we are leaving our mark on our sons.

I think our Father enjoys seeing that we look just like Him. He wants the love in our marriage to be a reflection of His love. I can just imagine Him whispering to me, *Let your husband off the hook. Rain down My mercy on him. Gently put your arm around your husband and tell him everything will be all right. Do something for him so he doesn't have to. You've got your Father's eyes, your Father's hands, and your Father's heart, My child, and that pleases Me.*

Gary Chapman, author of the bestselling *The Five Love Languages*, saw a radical transformation in his marriage when he began following Jesus' example of sacrificial love.

> About four months into this new approach to marriage, I first had the thought, *You know, maybe I could have positive feelings for her again.* I hadn't had warm feelings for a long time. My feelings were those of hurt, anger, and bitterness...I was an angry man before I read the life of Jesus. But four months into following Jesus, I began to sense love feelings for my wife again. About six months into this new relationship, I looked at her and had the thought, *I wouldn't mind touching her again if I thought she would let me.* I wasn't about to ask, but I had the thought, *I wouldn't mind if she wouldn't mind.*
>
> At that juncture I knew our marriage was going to make it. We have now been walking this road for a long time. Throughout the years I have reached out to her, discovering and meeting her needs to the best of my ability. And she, in turn, has devoted her life to knowing and loving me. What has happened in our marriage is nothing short of miraculous.[4]

Ideas for Loving Unconditionally

- Say "I love you" every day.

- Don't ever say "I told you so."

- Practice grace and mercy. Remember you need the same from your husband.

- Say "I forgive you" and mean it.

- Don't point out his mistakes. Just fill in the gap.

- Ask God to show you ways to serve your husband.

- Do something on his to-do list.

- Remember a time when something that bugs you about your husband was the very thing you loved about your husband.

- Meditate on God's love for you.

- Make the verses of 1 Corinthians 13:4-8 a prayer for your marriage.

- Pray for your husband every day.

A Husband Needs a Wife Who Is Forgiving, Not Bitter

Imagine you're in a circular room. A ten-foot wall of solid bricks encloses you in an impenetrable fortress. The one thick door is bolted. This is what unforgiveness looks like in marriage. After a few minutes you feel around in your pockets and discover that you actually have the key to unlock the door. The key in your marriage to break free from this impenetrable fortress is forgiveness. Are you going to use the key?

We all face many obstacles to love in marriage, but unforgiveness is one of the strongest. Unforgiveness keeps you and your husband as prisoners locked away from each other's intimacy.

"Love...does not take into account a wrong suffered" (1 Corinthians 13:4-5). How is this possible? Only with God's love pouring through you. Only by going honestly to the Lord and offering a heart that wants to please God more than it wants to be right, justified, hurt, or angry. This love doesn't dwell on past hurts or bring up past offenses in the heat of a fight. The New International Version renders 1 Corinthians 13:4-5 this way: "Love...keeps no record of wrongs."

Marriage has no room for scorekeeping. My friend Amy says of her marriage, "I love Mike with all my heart, and I honestly don't keep track of who's right or wrong. I don't remind him when he has screwed things up in the past, I don't nag him about past wrongdoings, I don't bring up the past in a present disagreement; I just move on. I don't even remember them!" This is a woman who has practiced forgiveness until it's become a habit for her. Forgiveness is now a part of her character.

Stormie Omartian's *The Power of a Praying Wife* has helped me renew my heart for loving my husband. She models a beautiful prayer of honesty and confession.

> Help me not to hold myself apart from [my husband] emotionally, mentally, or physically because of unforgiveness. Where either of us needs to ask forgiveness of the other, help us to do so. If there is something I'm not seeing that is adding to this problem, reveal it to me and help me to understand it. Remove any wedge of confusion that has created misunderstanding or miscommunication. Where there is behavior that needs to change in either of us, I pray You would enable that change to happen. As much as I want to hang on to my anger toward him because I feel it is justified, I want to do what *You* want. I release all those feelings to You. Give me a renewed sense of love for him and words to heal this situation.[5]

If this prayer reflects your heart, I encourage you to pray right now. Remember to turn to God so He can refresh your love for your husband.

Sheila and Tony faced a crisis in their marriage that they could resolve only through forgiveness. Sheila tells how Tony's dishonesty about their financial circumstances brought her to her knees.

> On our tenth wedding anniversary, I discovered that things in our marriage and life were not what they seemed. My husband, Tony, had been experiencing difficulties at work, including a dishonest partner and problems with the company's former owners. Quite by accident, I discovered that Tony had been writing rather large checks to his company from his personal checking account.
>
> When I confronted him, Tony admitted that things were much worse at work than he had let on, and that in fact he had been trying to cover up the situation by lying. He hadn't taken a salary since the beginning of the year. He had used all of our savings to pay for living expenses and to cover bills at the office. He had also used money from our retirement investments to prop up his

business. In four months, he had accumulated $20,000 in credit card bills. All in all, more than $200,000 was gone.

For me, this was the ultimate betrayal. Because of experiences in my past, this hit me harder than anything else would have—even an affair. I can honestly say that if I didn't have a relationship with Jesus, I would have left him that day. I will never forget the feelings—how devastated, and how utterly destitute and alone I felt.

Tony and I talked that night about the situation, this time much more calmly than before. As the days and weeks passed, I realized God was asking me to look at this from a different perspective...to think about just how horrible this had been for Tony. Each month he had seen something he had worked so hard for fall apart. He had to deal with *his* ultimate fears—fear of losing me if I found out or if he couldn't fix the problem. I knew I needed to forgive him, just as Jesus forgives us. Until I did, I couldn't move forward, and we couldn't move forward as a couple.

As the year progressed God continued to work on my heart. I began to see just how ugly unforgiveness is and how ugly I looked wearing it like a worn-out coat. On our eleventh wedding anniversary, exactly one year after I found out about our financial problems, I gave Tony a card with a folded piece of paper inside with the following three words: "I forgive you." That act set me free. And now I can say that we are stronger today than we were before. We make financial decisions as a team and are more open with each other about our thoughts and feelings. It hasn't been easy, but we are headed in the right direction.

Now I want to share this story from Tony's point of view. Hearing a man's point of view can help us understand what thoughts and feelings our own husbands might be struggling with.

When Sheila found out about the financial decisions I had been making, I finally realized that hiding them from her had been the same as lying to her. I also realized how poor the decisions had been. Once I admitted what I had been doing and saw her reaction, I felt horrible and began wondering how I could have made such a

terrible mistake. With tears, I repented before God, and
I believed He forgave me.

That was the turning point. Knowing that I was
on solid ground with God, I found strength to face my
problems. I left the partnership and started our current
business. I sought Sheila's forgiveness and told our older
daughters the facts. I spent time determining what
safeguards I could build into my life so this would not
happen again. I learned about God's forgiveness very
quickly, and I still marvel at the work He has done in
me and our family.

I am thankful for Sheila's and Tony's honesty about such a hard time
in their marriage. Unconditional love, as Sheila and Tony learned to give
each other, looks at the problem full in the face and says, "I choose to
forgive you. From this day forward I will not hold this against you."

What About My Husband?

In this book we're focusing on the wife's role, but we're always
tempted to think, *What about my husband? Isn't he supposed to do
the right thing too?* Yes, husbands are commanded to "love [their]
wives, just as Christ also loved the church and gave Himself up for her"
(Ephesians 5:25). That's a high calling for a husband! My obedience to
God, however, cannot be determined by my husband's actions. I am
responsible for my own choices. God will work on my husband. I can
also lovingly communicate my thoughts and feelings to my husband.
That's one way intimacy is built. But again, I am responsible for my
obedience to the Lord.

Satan whispers lies that if we forgive, our husbands will get away
with treating us wrong. Or if we forgive, we'll be hurt. Or "I've tried
this, and it doesn't work." Believing these lies creates hardened, bitter
hearts in us. Run from these lies. Don't let them latch on to your heart.
Their toxin will poison your marriage.

Love Your Husband by Praying for Him

In 15 years of marriage, I have certainly seen things in Scott that

I've wanted to change. I've made many mistakes of criticizing, nagging, and generally trying to change him. Of course, this didn't work! As I explained in the first chapter, I finally began acting wiser by praying for him. Unfortunately, I began by telling God how He needed to change Scott. Gradually, however, God helped me see that *I* needed to change. My selfish prayers gave way to requests that reflected my true love for Scott. The miracle of prayer is that God uses it to change me and give me His perspective of my marriage.

The most loving thing a wife can do for her husband is to pray every day for him.

As a wife I am privileged to partner with God in lavishing many different types of love on my husband. Loving my husband as a friend, romancing him, enjoying physical intimacy, and serving him are the colors of love I can use to paint a beautiful, multidimensional portrait of marriage.

PRAYER GUIDE

Dear Lord,

Thank You for loving me and empowering me to love others with Your love. Help me to be a reflection of Your love to my husband, to be Your heart and hands that reach out to him in love. Thank You that in the committed love my husband and I share, I am free to love him in all the ways You created love. Show me how he needs to be loved and give me a willingness to love him the way he will most feel loved. Help me to be honest with myself, my husband, and You, Lord, about any unforgiveness I'm holding onto. Help me to be forgiving so my love for my husband will flow freely. Renew and refresh our love for one another. I ask this in Your Son's name. Amen.

5

The Two Biggies:
Submission and Respect

When I was a young Christian, I would get very emotional and even angry when I heard any teaching about submitting to a husband. I simply did not get it, nor did I want to. Submission was completely contrary to any way of living I'd previously known.

Before I became a Christian, I was definitely my own master. I very much had a sense of entitlement and snubbed authority and rules. I can remember being a teenager and parking in a no parking zone, thinking I'd just run into a store quickly and get right back out before anyone noticed. Well, a policeman was standing nearby writing parking tickets for the other vehicles parked in the no parking zone. He graciously warned me to move my car before he wrote me a ticket.

Believe it or not, I completely ignored him. I just kept walking right into the store, and when I got back I had a ticket on my car to show for my rebellion.

Walk According to the Spirit

I had strong "flesh patterns" of rebellion to authority of any kind, so when I became a Christian, God had some substantial work to do in me! Scripture tells me that as a Christian I "do not walk according to the flesh but according to the Spirit" (Romans 8:4). The flesh is "that part of you which was trained to live independently of God before you met Christ…You still have memories, habits, conditioned responses, and thought patterns ingrained in your brain which prompt you to focus on your own interests."[1]

As a Christian wife I can choose to serve my flesh or choose to serve Christ. Each time I make the choice to serve Christ, I am ingraining new habits, new patterns of behavior, enabling me to experience the joy and freedom that come from obeying Him.

A Husband Needs a Wife Who Is Submissive

As I've talked to women and men about marriage, I've discovered that submission may be the most misunderstood concept in marriage. Submission has gotten a bad rap in our society. The word pushes our buttons and can make us see red. After all, our culture encourages independence, doing your own thing, and a me-first mentality. Submission doesn't fit in with those concepts, does it? Remember that Satan is our enemy, and he seeks to destroy what God created to be good.

Because this is such a misunderstood topic, let's take a moment to pray that we'll understand what God means by submission. Remember reading in chapter 1 about surrendering your marriage, *all* of your marriage, to God? Remember my suggestion that you pray with your palms facing up to symbolize surrendering your marriage? Can you do that again as you pray now? As you read this prayer, please make it your own prayer.

> *Dear Lord, I know that Your Word commands me to*
> *be submissive to my husband. Lord, please give me a right*
> *understanding of this concept. Help me to understand*

*what You mean by submission in marriage. Reveal to
me any lies I believe about submission. Open the eyes
of my heart to the truth. Then give me a heart that is
willing to submit to my husband. I ask these things in
Your name. Amen.*

Remembering that submission is *God's* idea and *God's* command
is very helpful. God commands wives to be submissive to their husbands: "Wives, be subject to your own husbands, as to the Lord. For
the husband is the head of the wife, as Christ also is the head of the
church, He Himself being the Savior of the body. But as the church
is subject to Christ, so also the wives ought to be to their husbands in
everything" (Ephesians 5:22-24). The New International Version uses
the word *submit* rather than *be subject*.

When I am submissive to my husband, I am doing first and foremost
what God wants me to do.

Submission Is Not...

First, let's understand what submission is not.

- Submission does not imply that the male is superior and
  the female is inferior. "God created man in His own
  image, in the image of God He created him; male and
  female He created them" (Genesis 1:27). We are unique
  and different from one another on purpose, as God
  designed and planned.

- Submission is not obeying your husband out of fear.

- It's not going along with things to gain an advantage to
  control or manipulate your husband.

- Submission does not mean that a wife says "Yes, dear" to
  whatever her husband suggests.

- Submission does not mean a wife and her husband never
  argue or that she never says anything that makes her
  husband mad.

- It does not mean that she closes her eyes to sin just for the

sake of keeping peace. You will sometimes need to speak
the truth in love to your husband, just as he will need to
do to you. In this way a husband and wife sharpen one
another and help one another become more Christlike.

One distortion of submission is to think wives can never disagree
with or reprove their husbands. This is simply not true! In chapter 3
we learned that God designed you to be your husband's helper. You
and your husband are partners, a team. Your personality and gifts
complement your husband's makeup. You can give your husband
input in a loving, kind, and thoughtful manner. Submission leads you
to sometimes say, "Honey, I'm not sure I agree with your decision, but
I will really try to support you."

We are always subject first to God's commandments, so if a husband
wants his wife to participate in a sinful activity, the wife has to say no to
sin. A husband might ask a wife to disobey God in many ways, especially
if he's not a Christian himself. He might not want her to go to church
or to take her children to church. He might want her to participate in
drunkenness or pornography. In these situations a wife must say no to
her husband. By lovingly saying no, she can demonstrate her desire to
be the best helper for her husband she can be.

A Right Understanding of Submission

So now let's understand what submission is. Being subject to
my husband means choosing to yield to my husband's authority. My
dictionary says that submission is "the act of yielding or surrendering
to the will or authority of another." God tells us what the chain of
command is to be in our family. In a husband and wife partnership, the
husband leads, and the wife follows. This chain of command provides a
family with order and responsibility. Paul addresses this responsibility
in 1 Corinthians 11:3: "But I want you to understand that Christ is the
head of every man, and the man is the head of a woman, and God is
the head of Christ."

Note that Ephesians 5:22 explains that when you submit to your
husband, you're really submitting to the Lord. One friend said that what
helps her to submit is to imagine that Jesus is standing right behind

her husband. She imagines herself looking right at Jesus as she tells her husband she'll follow his request.

Next, submission is best understood with the whole counsel of Scripture. The concept is woven throughout the pages of Scripture. The moment I became a Christian, I chose to submit to Jesus Christ as my Lord and Savior. In Ephesians 5:21 Christians are told to "be subject to one another." Submission is a vital part of being a Christian. Sometimes when I'm having trouble with submission to my husband, I realize that really I'm struggling with submitting to God in other areas of my life.

The greatest and most encouraging example of submission in Scripture is the relationship between God the Father, Jesus Christ the Son, and the Holy Spirit. Within the Trinity we see the practice of submission. Jesus Christ the Son submits to the Father: "My food is to do the will of Him who sent Me and to accomplish His work" (John 4:34). The Holy Spirit submits as well: He "will not speak on His own initiative, but whatever He hears, He will speak" (John 16:13).

Submission in Action

Submission is lived out in marriage in the small and big choices of everyday life. I'll share with you one little example from my own marriage that surprised me and opened my eyes to how Scott interprets my actions. One day Scott was throwing away something and saw a soda can in the trash. He got the can out of the garbage and with frustration in his voice asked me if I had thrown the can away. Of course, he knew I'd done it, and I knew he was irritated. So I admitted that yes, I'd thrown away the can and added that it wasn't a big deal. He explained that to him it was a big deal. He had told me numerous times that recycling was important to him, and by throwing that can away, I seemed to not care about his wishes.

Well, just writing this makes it sound so trivial! But marriage is made up of many small moments, many opportunities for us to honor our husbands. We live out our submission by our actions, the way we speak to our husbands, our tone of voice, and even our body language. We show our submission when we accept our husband's leadership and preferences in raising children, spending money, and keeping the house cleaned. Submission is choosing not to say or do something you know irritates your husband. It's choosing to ask your husband before you make a purchase, even if you know he probably won't want you to spend the money. It's not pushing and nagging and manipulating until you wear out your husband and get your own way.

You may live out your submission when your husband is led to go to a new church, even when that means you leave behind many good friends. Submission is yielding to his leadership when he wants to switch jobs, go back to school, or move to a new city.

Holly tells a story of how submitting to her husband blessed her and her family:

> When Dan and I married, we built a beautiful house in our hometown, and that was where I thought we'd stay for the rest of our lives. But after several years, Dan began sharing his career aspirations with me more frequently. His dream job was at his bank's headquarters in another state. I was not interested—I was very fearful of moving away from my family and friends and being homesick forever.
>
> I clearly remember the day that God placed a life-changing thought in my mind. Dan and I were driving on a beautiful country road near our home, when the Lord spoke through and for me as I simply and calmly said to Dan, "I'll be open-minded to the possibility of moving away." I was actually surprised that I had said it, but I felt very much at peace.
>
> Dan said very little until three weeks later. He came home one day and proudly told me that he had applied for a promotion at work, a promotion that would mean a move to another state.
>
> I was confident that God knew exactly what He was doing. By obeying my husband and following his plan for our lives, I was actually obeying God. God knew what was best for our family and for Dan's career path. It was not easy for me to submit to Dan's wish. I shed many, many tears for several months.
>
> But God did not disappoint us! We have not regretted a day that we've lived in our new hometown. Dan and I have grown closer, our relationship with God has increased to a new level of

maturity, and our kids have learned to handle change. God had even led me to co-lead a Bible study that helps women deal with the trials and tribulations of relocating. God's plan is always for our good if we have the courage to obey in faith.

It's Your Choice

As Holly's story illustrates, submission is always a matter of choice to yield your way, your rights, and your preferences to your husband. It's a way of trusting that God's commands for you and your marriage are for your good and for your protection. When we keep our eyes on God, our Audience of One, we will be able to do what He wants us to do.

Think for a few moments about what might be keeping you from submitting to your husband. Here are a few barriers that I've experienced: fear, pride, wanting to be in control, thinking I'm right and know best, having something to prove, and selfishness.

In chapter 4 we looked at some verses about love: "Love is patient… is not arrogant, does not act unbecomingly; it does not seek its own, is not provoked…bears all things, believes all things, hopes all things, endures all things" (1 Corinthians 13:4-7). The obstacles I've faced are exactly opposite of the way God wants us to love our husbands. So do you see how submitting to your husband is one way to love him?

When we started this book, we saw that what a husband needs from his wife is not for her to apply a formula or a quick fix. Instead, he needs her to engage in a step-by-step journey with God, taking one step at a time, following His lead in her marriage. God may lead you in a way that is unique to your situation. Listen to what my friend Jill decided to do in her marriage.

Jill and Tom both had good jobs, she as a teacher and he as a computer programmer. Like many young couples, however, they had no financial plan. They managed to stay above water because they both had good incomes, but they spent every penny and had no long-term plans. They never discussed a budget and never consulted with one another about purchases.

Neither one of them wanted to take charge of the finances because the task seemed so overwhelming. But eventually, probably just because Jill had a little more free time, she ended up in charge of paying the bills, balancing the checkbook, and creating a budget.

Jill liked to shop, so on one hand, being in charge of the finances suited her. She knew what she could spend without overdrawing their checking account, so that's what she did. Overall, however, she hated the responsibility. She didn't think she was very good at it, and she knew that her analytical husband would do a better job. She tried to at least involve Tom in their financial record keeping, but he wanted nothing to do with it. He didn't want to think about it. He just wanted the money to be available when he wanted to buy something, and he wanted Jill to make sure of that.

Jill really felt that as the leader of the family, Tom needed to be in charge of the finances. But regardless of how much she begged him to take over, he refused. Although she was going along with her husband's wishes because she thought she was supposed to, she became distraught and resentful.

As their lives and marriage became more filled with stress and strife, Jill cried out to God. She didn't want her marriage to be in the place that it was. They both loved each other, but this conflict was consuming them and draining the life out of their marriage. She began to see that God wanted Tom to be in charge of their finances. She was very relieved, but she was confused about what to do because Tom clearly didn't want the responsibility.

With much prayer, she approached Tom. She told him that she had been praying, and she sensed that God might want him to take over the finances. She asked if he would pray about it too. He got extremely angry and ended the conversation, but Jill continued to pray. She let a week pass, and then she approached Tom again. She got the same reaction.

Finally, she decided to take a radical step. She approached Tom again in a loving and respectful manner and handed the finances over to him. She told Tom that she really believed this was an area he needed to grow in, that he needed to take financial leadership in their family, and that the burden was too much for her to bear alone.

She told him she would no longer be in charge of the finances. She handed him all the paperwork and let him know she'd be glad to show him how she organized things. I wish I could say that Tom quickly realized his responsibility and graciously stepped up. But in fact, they had even more conflict in their marriage. Their financial situation spiraled downward. Tom missed many payments, and they even had a car repossessed.

Jill remained prayerful and loving to Tom while pouring out her heart and tears to God. They saw a Christian counselor when the word *divorce* entered their conversations. After about a year, their marriage began to turn the corner. It was a long, long year for Jill. Many times she questioned whether she had heard God's guidance correctly. Letting their finances get so out of control seemed nonsensical. But God continued to affirm that in the long run this would be best for their marriage. And it was. Tom eventually accepted the leadership role in their family, and Jill became better at following him. Jill and Tom now have a marriage that pleases God and brings joy to both of them.

What do you think about that story? What would you have done? Honestly, I don't know what I would have done. I do remember thinking that Jill had incredible faith. She was certainly an example to me of a godly woman wanting to do God's will. She was an example to me of trusting God's wisdom, not her own. Many Christian women follow the ways of the world rather than God's way in their roles as wives.

Sometimes we wives take over by default. We don't see our husbands stepping up to the plate to lead the family, so we think we have to step in. As Jill and Tom's story shows us, sometimes a man doesn't lead because he doesn't know how to, he fears failure, or he just chooses the easy way of letting his wife be in charge. He becomes more and more passive in an area where God wants him to lead.

As a helper, one of my jobs is to help my husband in the role God created for him, one of leadership, protection, and provision for his family. Jill knew that the best thing she could do as her husband's helper was to let him lead. I admire the way Jill trusted God. She prayed, and God showed her this was an area Tom needed to grow in. She took a giant leap of faith when she relinquished the finances into Tom's hands.

She watched Tom's stumbling steps and felt the heat of the challenge, but she persevered. Her example was certainly an example to me, and I hope it is to you too.

A Husband Needs a Wife Who Shows Him Respect

In chapter 4 we discussed the love your husband needs. In this chapter we've discussed submission, and now let's look at the attitude of respect. God's instruction manual, the Bible, tells us "the wife must see to it that she respects her husband" (Ephesians 5:33).

The three attitudes of love, submission, and respect go hand in hand. Respect is the most loving and submissive attitude a wife can show her husband. If we want our husbands to feel loved, we need to make sure we are showing them respect. This is hard for women to grasp! In general women are nourished by love while men, on the other hand, are filled up and ignited by respect.

What Is Unconditional Respect?

Wives, we must show our husbands respect whether we feel like it or not! Think about that. Our husbands do not have to earn our respect. For me and maybe for you too, that's a pretty novel concept. I'd have to say that during most of our marriage I showed Scott respect if I thought he deserved it. God turns that idea upside down. God wants us to respect our husbands because they're our husbands.

Many women find the idea of unconditional *love* completely acceptable and biblical; however, we tend to reject the idea of unconditional *respect*. We tend to think our husbands must earn our respect. This is not God's commandment! God's command for us to respect our husbands does not depend on anything they do, just as the command for them to love us is not conditional.

> Unconditional respect works because it is from God Himself. God could have commanded wives to agape-love their husbands. He does not. That silence is significant. So, this is a faith and obedience venture. If a wife loves and reveres the Lord, she will seek to love her husband the way God says, unconditionally respectful in tone,

facial expression, and deeds. Truthfully, this is an issue of obedience to the woman following Christ.[2]

Talking the language of love is much easier for me than talking the language of respect. Sometimes I act disrespectfully without ever intending to. One day when we were planning a trip, my husband and I had a conversation that sounded something like this:

> Scott: Melanie, let's look online at some hotels and book one.
>
> Melanie: Honey, why don't you do that. You're so much better at that than I am. I know whatever you choose will be great.
>
> Scott: No way. As soon as I choose one, you'll tell me something's wrong with it.
>
> Melanie: No, really, I promise I won't. (I walked away to clean up the kitchen while Scott went online.)
>
> Scott (an hour later): Melanie, let me show where we'll be staying. We've got a suite...
>
> Melanie (interrupting): Does it have two separate beds or is one of them a pull-out bed? Those pull-outs can be uncomfortable.
>
> Scott (with controlled frustration in his voice): Well, if you'd let me finish talking, I could tell you that it has two separate beds. We're only five minutes away from Disneyland, and we have free breakfast each morning.
>
> Melanie: Oh, we don't have a view from our hotel room of Disneyland? That would have been fun; we could watch the fireworks from there.
>
> Scott (with much more frustration in his voice): See what I mean? You had to find something wrong!
>
> Melanie: No, no; it's fine. It's no big deal. I was just mentioning it. You don't have to get mad at me for saying one little thing.
>
> Scott: Just forget it.
>
> Melanie: What are you so mad about?
>
> Scott: Nothing.

Have you ever had a conversation like this? Suddenly, your husband is frustrated, angry, or shut down. If we see our husbands showing these emotions, they probably feel disrespected. Now notice that our husbands can feel disrespected even when we have no intention of making them feel that way. In the conversation I had with Scott, I felt like I was just asking two little questions. Why did that make him feel so angry?

Why does your husband get angry when you don't take his advice on something you think seems trivial? Why does he get frustrated when you remind him to fix the broken faucet? Why does he get mad when you tell him as you're walking out the door that the baby needs a bottle in two hours? To a man these statements communicate distrust and disrespect.

We might be tempted to think our husbands should be less sensitive, but we have to consider respect from a man's point of view just as we expect him to look at love from our perspective. We want our husbands to be sensitive to the statements that seem unloving to us. For example, if you ask your husband, "Do these pants make me look fat?" and he answers yes, you will feel unloved and hurt. The answer you're looking for, of course, is "No, honey, you look beautiful." We want our husbands to be sensitive to us in the same way they want us to be sensitive to them.

> Considering that most men appear to be highly sensitive to disrespect—including seeing disrespect where none is intended—I would argue that it is not the average man who needs to be less sensitive to a woman's words, but the average woman who needs to be more sensitive to her man's feelings.[3]

Start practicing respect today. Show your husband a respectful attitude. Use the R word (respect) as often as you can. Tell him you respect him. Many women will use the word *love*, when what a man is longing to hear is that his wife respects him. "I respect the way you handled that situation. I respect the way you work hard every day. I respect how smart you are about our finances. I respect the decision you made. I respect how you can fix things around the house. I respect how safe you make me feel."

Respect him by trusting his decisions. When he makes a final decision as the leader in your home, can you go along with it without asking any questions or trying to tweak it a bit? Respect him by following his wishes even when he's not around to see, even when God is the only One who will know! Respect him by not showing outright defiance. Respect him by not taking matters into your own hands when you think he's moving too slowly. Respect that he is different from you and does things differently from the way you might do them. Respect him by listening while not doing anything else.

Lisa came dangerously close to abandoning her marriage. She shares how practicing unconditional respect dramatically transformed her marriage.

God began to convict me about my attitude toward Mike. I learned that God's Word said to respect my husband unconditionally, so I vowed I would obey God. Acting respectfully when I did not feel like it, however, was not easy. Several times I went into my garage and cried out to God for His help. I begged God to intervene because my fleshly desires were at times too strong to control. I relied heavily on God's promise from His Word: "I can do all things through Christ who strengthens me" (Philippians 4:13).

God never failed me. He spoke clearly to Mike's heart, more clearly than my ranting and raving. Amazingly enough, Mike and I argued less frequently and apologized to one another more frequently. My relationship with God grew deeper than ever before, and Mike's hunger for the Lord began to grow. He made Christian friends, joined a men's Bible study, and began attending a Sunday school class. He became the spiritual leader in our home in the way I had hoped for.

He then stood before a group of more than 100 people and testified that my faith in God and my obedience to unconditional respect allowed God to change our hearts and our marriage. I was blessed beyond measure. I felt as if God had wrapped me in His arms and whispered, "Well done, good and faithful servant."

Our marriage is still a work in progress, and God's mercies are new every day. I can honestly say that the pain of laying down my pride and not requiring Mike to earn my respect have set me free.

God did it all. Lisa is now leading Bible studies about marriage and sharing her testimony of how God transformed her marriage. She is such an example of perseverance and faith. I love the way Mike gave her so much credit in changing his heart. Wow.

What do you think your husband would say about the way you submit to him? Does he think you respect him? What do your children see you modeling in these areas? What does God think about the way you submit to and respect your husband? Talk to your heavenly Father in prayer.

Reaping and Sowing

The concept of reaping and sowing is found throughout the Bible. "For whatever a man sows, this he will also reap" (Galatians 6:7). In the gardening world, if I plant a tomato seed, I expect to see a tomato plant bearing tomatoes, not a cucumber plant bearing watermelons!

Reaping and sowing also has spiritual implications for our marriages. Whatever I sow into my marriage, I can expect to reap. If I'm sowing sinful qualities such as selfishness or disrespect, I can expect to reap a marriage lacking the qualities I long for. If I want a marriage filled with unconditional love, intimacy, friendship, laughter, passion, and unity, then I must sow into my marriage the actions God expects of a wife, such as submission and respect. Obedience to God in our marriages brings the blessings we long for.

So often we want to experience the blessings of obedience without obeying. We want fulfilled marriages without being excellent wives. We want personal satisfaction and joy, but we want the option of dragging our heels whenever we feel like it. We want to know God's will for our lives, but we're too busy to sit at His feet and discover just what that is. Many want to be godly, but few are willing to be obedient. Yet obedience is the very thing on which abiding hinges. Obedience opens the door to an understanding of who God is and shows us more fully what His will for our lives is.[4]

Jennifer is discovering the blessings of obeying God in her marriage:

> I was spending some time with God today, and it occurred to me how good it feels to obey Him. I remember when I was young and the world revolved around me. The neat thing is that as my relationship with God grows and my love toward Him grows, the obedience is no longer about following God out of duty. I've found that it is a freedom and honor to hear His voice and to obey Him. It feels so much better. It's a sweet, wise, secure feeling. It's obedience out of love and trust. God is so good!

PRAYER GUIDE

Dear Lord,

I pray that I will walk in Your Spirit, not my sinful flesh. Each time I obey You, Lord, create and strengthen new patterns of behavior that glorify You. I pray today that You will reveal to me where I have been unwilling to shower my husband with the attitudes of submission and respect. Remind me, Lord, that when I submit to my husband, ultimately I'm submitting to You. Reveal to me any demands I've made on my husband to earn respect. Give me the courage to ask forgiveness of my husband, for when I sin against him, I've sinned against You.

Lord, being submissive and respectful can be hard to do in marriage. Help me to obey You and not to walk in the flesh or listen to Satan's lies. Where Satan has gained ground in my marriage, I take back the territory of my marriage by submitting to and respecting my husband. I know that obeying You will set us free to experience joy, closeness, friendship, and passion as You've intended for us. I love You, Lord, and trust Your commandments for our marriage. I pray this in Jesus' name. Amen.

6

Attitude Adjustment

When my sons were young, we played outside as much as possible. One particular day we had been outside for a couple of hours when I gave the five-minute warning for going inside. The minute I announced this, my normally calm kindergartner, Zachary, decided he didn't like the plan I'd laid out. His buddy Joey had just arrived on the scene, and he wanted to stay outside.

The power struggle began. He grabbed his bike's handlebars with a death grip and refused to budge. Of course, I had to come up with a consequence for such outright defiance. I told him he needed to go inside immediately. In addition, he would not be playing his Nintendo that night. He glared at me and I at him, and then he stomped inside.

I stayed outside for a few minutes to visit with Joey's mother, and suddenly the front door flew open. I saw a little hand toss out a piece of paper, and then the front door slammed shut. Curious, I picked up the paper and read the words written by my little kindergartner: "Mom is a dog." I couldn't help but smile, even though they were words of defiance, for I knew these words were among the few words he could spell.

I'm much like my little Zachary. I may be outwardly obedient in my actions but all the while thinking, *My husband is a jerk* (the wife's version of "Mom is a dog"). I am sure God wants to say to me what I often say to my kids: *You need an attitude adjustment!*

In the previous two chapters we looked at three commandments in Scripture for wives to love, submit to, and respect their husbands. In this chapter we'll continue to look at the heart of a godly wife. As you read, ask God to show you which of these attitudes your husband most needs to feel loved. Ask Him to reveal other attitudes not discussed here. Be willing to go there!

A Husband Needs a Wife Who Is Thankful, Not Ungrateful

> Rejoice always; pray without ceasing; in everything give thanks; for this is God's will for you in Christ Jesus (1 Thessalonians 5:16-18).

Last year we decided to take a "real" family vacation to Disneyland in California instead of using our vacation time to visit our family. We thought it would be our kids' dream come true. Well, it wasn't—not by a long shot! After about only two hours of being at Disneyland, my five-year-old son, Tyler, had had enough. He stopped dead in his tracks, crossed his arms, and exclaimed, "This is stupid! All we do is walk around and wait in these stupid lines and it's hot and it's not fun and I'm not doing it anymore!" I wanted to jerk his arm off and snatch him bald-headed! We'd gone to a considerable effort and spent plenty of money to make sure the kids had a fun vacation. Scott and I sat him down and lectured him about being thankful, loaded him up with some sugar and caffeine, and off we went to have more fun!

I wonder if God feels the same way we as parents did that day: *You're in Disneyland, child. Be thankful! Stop your whining!*

Are you thankful in your marriage? Are you thankful for your marriage? Are you thankful for your husband? Have you thanked God for your husband? Do you thank your husband for all that he is and does for your family? Remember the little song from childhood that goes, "Count your many blessings, name them one by one"? Keeping a thankful journal where each day you write down five things you're thankful for can really help you avoid an ungrateful attitude. Be specific as you're thanking God. For example, instead of thanking God for a husband who is "great with the kids," thank God for a husband who wrestles with the boys, prays with them, and plays sports with them. Count your blessings!

My husband really needs to hear me thank him for his work. He needs to know I do not take for granted his hard work each day. I need to verbalize my thanks over and over and over. I also need to teach my children to be thankful for his hard work. They need to hear me thanking my husband, and they need to realize that his hard work is what God uses to provide many material blessings.

Lysa TerKeurst tells a story in *Capture His Heart* of a woman who really understood the importance of a wife being thankful for her husband's work.

> I was at a church retreat once where a woman shared a song she wrote to esteem her husband. When she wrote it he was working in a hot dog stand, and she proudly called herself the woman lucky enough to have married the hot dog man. He was there when she shared the song, and he beamed with happiness. I don't know whatever became of the hot dog man and his wife, but I do know whatever that man chooses to do in his life he'll be successful. Not because of how much money he makes or how many degrees he may acquire but because he has a woman who believes in him.[1]

Sometimes I'm surprised when Scott tells me he feels unappreciated. Inside I feel thankful for him, but I just haven't done a very good job of expressing it. A man who feels unappreciated is like a balloon whose air has escaped. When he feels unappreciated, he might also feel defeated and unmotivated. These feelings lead a man to feel as if he leads a life of drudgery. A wife can help "fill his balloon" with her words of appreciation.

Ideas for Thanking Your Husband

- Thank God for giving you your husband.

- Each day tell your husband "thank you" for something specific about his character or something specific he does for you or your family.

- Let him overhear you telling someone else how much you appreciate him.

- Have your children make a thank-you sign or write a thank-you note to their dad.

- When he comes home at the end of the workday, thank him with a warm smile, hug and kiss, and promises for more later.

- When he walks in the door, don't bombard him with questions, complaints, reports of your day, and matters with the kids. Let him unwind.

- Bake his favorite treat or make his favorite meal.

- Tell him every day, "I love you," and "I'm so glad I'm married to you."

A Husband Needs a Wife Who Is Content, Not Complaining

> Do all things without grumbling (Philippians 2:14).

A husband needs a wife who is content, not complaining. Most men I know and have talked to about this subject really want their wives to be content and will do what they can to make sure they are. However, sometimes knowing what a wife needs to be content isn't easy. One day you seem to need a day away from the kids, the next day you need time with him, and the next day you need more money to buy the kids school clothes. A husband might think that regardless of what he does, he cannot do enough. You are not satisfied! What a heavy burden for a man to carry! This is not a fair burden for you to put on your husband.

A wife's contentment must come from the Lord. Her satisfied attitude flows out of her relationship with Him. A content wife knows God has provided for her salvation in the death and resurrection of Jesus Christ. She knows God as her Jehovah-Jireh, her Provider; and she knows God as her El Shaddai, her All-Sufficient One. A content wife knows that "God will supply all [her] needs according to His riches in glory in Christ Jesus" (Philippians 4:19).

I can't help but think about the ancient Israelites, who are infamous for their complaining. Deuteronomy 1:2 tells us the journey to the promised land was actually an 11-day trip, but the Israelites' discontented hearts turned their journey into 40 years. Might we possibly do something similar in our marriages? Are we missing so many of the blessings God intended for us in our marriages because we complain?

Ideas for Showing a Contented Attitude

- Don't think or wish you were married to someone else.

- Don't compare him to other men.

- Don't say you wish you had enough money to buy a nicer house or (you fill in the blank!).

- Be involved in the finances. Know where your family stands financially.

- Ask God for what you need, and ask God to make you content.

- Thank God specifically for the tangible and intangible blessings in your life.

- Assume the best and give your husband the benefit of the doubt.

A Husband Needs a Wife Who Is Cheerful, Not Downhearted

> A cheerful heart has a continual feast (Proverbs 15:15).

Women are the heart of the home, and our attitudes set the emotional temperature in our families. A wife's positive attitude can permeate her home like the sweet aroma of freshly picked flowers, or her negative attitude can pollute her home like stinky garbage.

A positive attitude fills our homes when we choose to be cheerful instead of down or complaining. Being cheerful is not natural for me. I've called my mind-set many things, such as realistic or practical, but really it's just a negative outlook. I used to believe that if I don't act the way I feel, I'm being a fake or a hypocrite.

But God has shown me plain and simple that to act with a negative attitude is sinful. I've seen how my negative attitude can affect everyone around me. God is also showing me that sometimes I need to act first, and then the feelings will follow.

Galatians 2:20 tells me that Christ lives in me, so I have His mind-set in me. When my mind is set on God, I have God's eternal perspective. A shift in our minds can make a powerful difference in our attitudes, as Lysa TerKeurst's story demonstrates.

> If you had longed for children and then suddenly today you were blessed with toys to organize, bedtime stories to tell, and little messy hands to wipe, would this be your greatest day ever?
>
> If you were paralyzed and then today you suddenly could climb the stairs, run after a toddler, jump up and down cheering for your teen, would this be your greatest day ever?
>
> If you had no husband, then today God gave you a

man to do laundry for, help fold his collar over his tie, cook his favorite meal, and wrap your arms around at night as you fall asleep, would this be your greatest day ever?

If you had no home, then suddenly you were blessed with dishes to wash, beds to make, weeds to pull and floors to sweep, would this be your greatest day ever?[2]

Ask God to show you when your husband can especially benefit from your cheerfulness. Phone conversations are the biggest challenge for me. My husband travels quite a bit, as do so many husbands, so a phone conversation can be an important lifeline during an absence. My first reaction when I talk to Scott is to list everything that's gone wrong that day and even to add in some things that I think will go wrong as the day progresses. This has become a really bad habit for me. I am working—one phone conversation at a time—at being more positive! I will have plenty of time later to include Scott in problems that really need his attention. When he's on the road missing me and our sons, he just needs to hear we love him, miss him, and appreciate his hard work.

So what about you? When will your cheerfulness most likely minister to your husband?

Ideas for Showing a Cheerful Attitude

- Look at your husband with a happy smile, not a scornful scowl.
- Greet him as if you've been waiting for him all day, not as if he's an intrusion to whatever you're doing.
- Teach your children to drop everything when Daddy comes home so they can give him a big hug.
- Call him to tell him something that will cheer him.
- Do everyday tasks with a positive attitude.
- Rejoice always.
- Laugh hard and often.
- Remember God loves a cheerful giver (2 Corinthians 9:7).

A Husband Needs a Wife Who Is
Flexible, Not Controlling

> There is a way which seems right to a man, but its
> end is the way of death (Proverbs 14:12).

I have just returned from standing in the rain, trying to get our new puppy, Emma, to go potty. No luck. I'll be back out there shortly. Tending to her needs will take away from what I think I need to be doing—writing! So I'm patting myself on the back for agreeing with my husband to get this second dog. You see, I thought I was doing a great job at being accommodating when we got our first dog, Jenna, two years ago. Agreeing to add this second dog has required a lot of prayer. However, I can honestly say that seeing how happy the two dogs make my husband makes me happy.

When we are flexible in marriage, we're really surrendering to God. We have plenty of opportunities to practice flexibility in marriage. Consider these scenarios. You finally have time to work on your scrapbook, but your husband wants you to go walk the dog with him. You're in bed reading your book, and your husband wants to be romantic. Your husband is watching football, and you'd like to run some errands, but you know he'd really love for you just to sit on the couch with him and enjoy the game A positive response can powerfully communicate your love and respect.

I can usually be more flexible by asking myself a simple question: Does this situation that I'm getting irritated or disturbed about really matter in the long run? Or does it just matter because I want to get my own way?

Renee Swope, speaker, author, and director of the Proverbs 31 Speaker Team, shares a story about a time when she chose to be flexible and how she was blessed because of her choice.

> My husband and I each needed some extra work time. So we decided J.J. would stay at his office late Monday night and go straight from work to his weekly Bible study. I would have dinner with our boys, make sure homework was done, and put

them to bed, and he'd be home around 10:30. Tuesday would be my work night…

Monday went just as planned. Tuesday came and the day whizzed by! It felt like only an hour had passed at work in the Proverbs 31 office before it was time to go home. Hurriedly, I stuffed my files with papers and put them in my briefcase, as a wave of anxiety swept over me. Then I remembered the plan and reminded myself that I could complete my work later, when J.J. got home.

My plans never became a reality. J.J. called at five o'clock and said he needed to work late. Much to my surprise, I didn't feel angry. I knew he didn't have control over the circumstances, so I told him I would adjust and spend the evening with the boys.

Although I didn't feel angry, I did feel anxious. As I hung up the phone with J.J. I looked at the files on my desk and reminded God of my plan for that evening. I made sure He was aware of what needed to be done and all the people who were waiting for my response. Before I could write God another mental memo or water my seeds of anxiety with worries, my spirit reminded my heart of the truth I know about God's plans. Thoughts gave way to an unexpected prayer. "Lord, I had plans for tonight; plans that would bring me peace and a sense of completion. But You know the plans You have for me; plans to prosper me, not to harm me; plans to give me a future that leads to hope. Obviously my plans were not Your plans, so please show me the plans You have for this night" (Jeremiah 29:11).

I never touched my files that evening. Instead the boys and I ordered pizza, cleaned the kitchen together, and folded clothes while we watched a family video. Our evening had an unusual sweetness as we sorted socks and snuggled on the couch.

God's plan was for me to be a helper to my husband, a mom to my kids, and a keeper of our home. When I surrendered to His plan, a peace that surpassed my understanding came over me. I had planned to find peace in getting things done, but God's peace came when my plans came undone and made room for the plans He had for me.[3]

Being flexible is a way to surrender your marriage to God, putting your rights, plans, and way of doings things on the altar. It's a way to die to yourself, as Christ modeled on the cross. Remember the suggestion of praying with open palms as a symbol of your surrender? Start each day with a prayer of submission of your plans for the day. Then when your husband makes a suggestion that might differ from your idea, you'll know you're ultimately accommodating God's plans.

One more thought: Being flexible in the small things will prepare you to be flexible in the larger issues of marriage. I met Cassie about five years ago in a women's Bible study at my church. She was quiet, but her facial expressions showed that she was soaking up and enjoying the teaching. I wished she would speak up, as I wanted to get to know her better. The day came when she finally responded aloud to a question. The question had something to do with why men behave a certain way, and this was her answer: "Because men are stupid!" We all looked at her in shock as she had finally spoken up, and of all things to say! Years later we are still laughing about that story. I tell it now only because my sweet friend has let God change her so much.

Cassie is a young mother of two with a third child on the way. For years her husband has been traveling over an hour each way to work. Nate has a great job, one where his skills and talents have been acknowledged and he has received promotions, so he really doesn't want to find another job closer to home. Recently they sold their home to move closer to Nate's work. Despite her reluctance to leave the support of her church and friends, Cassie has had such a gracious attitude toward her husband in this matter. Inside she's fearful of the change. After all, she'll soon have three little ones under the age of four at home, she's leaving the support of her friends, and she's venturing into the unknown. Cassie has agreed to this change because she is a young woman who loves God and loves her husband. She knows that she can trust God with her future and that in her obedience, she'll be blessed with a closer relationship with God and her husband.

Ideas for Being Flexible

- Respond with an enthusiastic "Yes!" or "Sure!" or "That's a great idea!"

- At the start of each day, ask God for His agenda and then look for His answer.

- When your husband takes care of a situation in a manner different from the way you would do it, don't correct him!

- Tell him that whatever he wants to do is great with you—and mean it!

- Assume the best about your husband.

- Let go of having to be right.

- Ask your husband, "What do you think?"

A Husband Needs a Wife Who Is Self-Controlled, Not Emotional

> But the fruit of the spirit is...self-control (Galatians 5:22-23).

I am sure some days Scott has felt as if he were navigating a path between the land mines of my emotions. One day I might be dealing with the drama of a bad hair day or lamenting that "I'm fat and nothing in my closet fits and I have nothing to wear." Maybe I'm feeling as if I just cannot take another day with the children, and I have to get away for a few hours. Or I'm fed up with my unsatisfying job where nobody appreciates me. Or my husband hasn't spent any time with me, and I'm feeling unloved.

On these overly emotional days, I feel as if Satan has set up camp in my home and is trying to take up permanent residence. If I respond to my out-of-control emotions, I am giving Satan a foothold in my marriage. If I realize that my emotions cannot determine my actions and ask God to control my emotions, then Christ is the center of my home, and He protects me from Satan's attack. "I know of no tool that the Enemy uses more effectively to lead us as women into bondage than our emotions. He does so by causing us to believe things about our emotions that just aren't true."[4]

Our husbands need to be able to depend on our stability and consistency without having to live in fear of what lies around the corner. Along our marriage journey we're going to have feelings of hurt, anger, and disappointment. Are we supposed to pretend we don't feel these things? Not at all. We need to take all these feelings to Jesus and be totally honest with Him. He knows us, and He knows our feelings. Read Psalms, and you will find expressions of every emotion possible. God made us to be emotional, but not to be ruled by our emotions.

Ugly, harsh, critical words are often the results of our uncontrolled emotions, so sometimes the best course of action is simply to say as little as possible. "When there are many words, transgression is unavoidable, but he who restrains his lips is wise" (Proverbs 10:19).

Don't set yourself up for failure in this area of self-control. In other words, know what makes you emotionally vulnerable and take practical steps to avoid those things. The number one thing I need in order to be emotionally stable is time with God. The second priority for me to be emotionally consistent is adequate sleep. I need eight hours of sleep as often as possible. However, even when I don't get that amount of sleep, I need to be careful not to use the lack as an excuse for ungodly behavior. I can, however, communicate with my husband that I'm tired and that I would really appreciate his help with the kids after dinner, for example. Exercise, nutrition, books you read, TV shows you watch, your schedule, and the company you keep can all affect your emotions. Ask God to reveal to you what tempts you to fluctuate emotionally. Ask Him also to show you what you need to do to remedy this situation.

Ideas for Being Self-Controlled

- Know your triggers and avoid them. If too much chocolate and caffeine make you irritable, cut back!

- Take a time-out for yourself before shouting ugly words.

- Shower your husband with grace and mercy, not judgment and criticism.

- If you can't say anything nice, don't say anything at all.

- Practice discipline in all areas of your life, not just in your marriage.

- Pour out your emotions to God.

A Husband Needs a Wife Who Is Encouraging, Not Critical

> Therefore encourage one another and build up one another, just as you also are doing (1 Thessalonians 5:11).

I have a picture of Scott when he was about seven years old. His grin is wide as he proudly displays a big fish he caught in a Minnesota lake. I love what this picture reminds me of: Inside each grown man is a little boy whose actions cry out for attention, recognition, and applause.

> Men will always gravitate toward the loudest applause. That's why they gravitate toward the softball league, the men's ministry, the gym, or the happy hour. It's why some keep reliving bygone days when they were the star of their football team and why others have to be pried away from their desks. They simply want to be in a place where they get the biggest cheers and the most frequent pats on the back.[5]

Our husbands are all grown up, but they still long for cheerleaders, not critics. They need us to be wives who give them encouragement, wives who help put the courage in them, wives who let them know we believe in them. Wendy has become more aware of her husband's need of her encouragement:

> I know that sometimes my husband feels that he has the weight of the world on his shoulders. His main concern is to take care of his family. Just a word of encouragement or support from me seems to push him to the top of the world instead of under it. He tries

so hard and does so much. When he starts feeling the pressure of everything weighing on him, I can just stop and tell him how wonderful he is or what a great job he does with the kids, and that pressure fades away. Just being sensitive to his needs is the biggest part of being my husband's helper.

One of the greatest gifts a wife can give her husband is the encouragement of his manhood. No book has helped me understand this more than John Eldredge's *Wild at Heart*. Eldredge explains that a man was created to be a man, so let him be a *man!* One of the greatest revelations in this book is that Christianity has perpetuated the wrong image of a Christian man as a "nice guy." Eldredge explains that in every man's heart is the desire "for a battle to fight, an adventure to live, and a beauty to rescue."[6]

In modern society a man will express his manhood in many ways: succeeding at work, being a leader among his peers, watching sports, playing sports, talking about sports, working on cars, working with tools, competing in everything and anything, working outside, driving a big truck or a tractor, wrestling with the kids, racing cars, hunting, fishing, getting dirty, and being smelly. Let him be a man. Encourage him to be a man. Enjoy his manliness.

A husband does not need a critic. He gets enough of that from the world and sometimes from his own self-doubts. "Every man feels that the world is asking him to be something he doubts very much he has it in him to be."[7] As my friend Lysa suggested in an e-mail: "Complete him where he falls short. Instead of criticizing him, step in and help fill in his gaps willingly."

When he shares his dreams, don't respond with "How in the world would we afford for you to do that?" Just listen and be his friend and his partner. He doesn't need you to rain on his parade. He doesn't need unsolicited advice. He doesn't need you to remind him that your way would have been better. And he doesn't need judgment when something he does goes south. He needs your arms open wide and an embrace that says no matter what, I love you, and I'm by your side.

Writer Elizabeth George has a great guideline for speaking about our husbands: "I have very few 'never's' in my life, but one primary 'never' is never speak critically or negatively about my husband to anyone."⁸ That's a guideline every wife needs to put into practice.

Ideas for Encouraging Your Husband

- Write him a note or send him an e-mail listing ten reasons you think he's "it on a stick."

- Verbally praise him in front of others, especially your children.

- Admire his muscles and strength.

- Go to his basketball or softball games and cheer the loudest.

- Respond to him in a way that lets him know you think he's the sexiest man alive.

- Make a promise to God to never, ever speak critically about your husband to anyone else.

- Encourage him with your quiet presence.

- Don't tease him about something that you know is a touchy subject.

- Tell him he's the best thing that ever happened to you.

A Husband Needs a Wife Who Is Gentle, Not Harsh

> A gentle answer turns away wrath, but a harsh word stirs up anger (Proverbs 15:1).

We know from 1 Peter 3:1-6 that God values the inner beauty of a woman, her gentle and quiet spirit. As I was discussing this verse with a male acquaintance, he shook his head and said, "My wife is like a sledgehammer. Nothing is gentle about her. She's like a runaway bus, and you just better get out of her way." If we're honest, I'm sure most of us can think of times when our manner and attitude have been more like the blows of a sledgehammer than soft caresses.

We can show our husbands gentleness in many ways—a soft touch, a sweet smile, a kind deed, and a caring tone of voice. We show gentleness when we are considerate, patient, understanding, not easily offended or irritated, and forgiving.

Think about the opposite of gentle—harsh, pushy, insistent, demanding, caustic, and argumentative. Are you more likely to respond to your husband in gentleness or harshness?

Sometimes I think we fear being gentle because we don't want to appear weak or vulnerable. That's a lie God doesn't want us to believe! In Isaiah 40:10-11 we see that God is both a mighty warrior and a tender shepherd. In the same way, a woman can be both gentle and strong. Consider the ways of a mother with her child; she is the one who scoops her child into her arms and hugs him tighter than tight, and she's also the one who is fiercely protective of her child's well-being.

Gentleness is part of being feminine, part of being a woman, and God made us distinctly different from men on purpose! God wants us to bring our gentleness to our marriages, to love our husbands with the tender love of God. Our tenderness woos our husbands and allows them to be vulnerable too.

Ideas for Practicing a Gentle Attitude

- Don't interrupt him, correct him, or nag him, especially around others.

- Ask a friend to hold you accountable—if she hears you speak in a harsh manner, ask her to tell you.

- Enjoy God's quiet presence and tender love.

- Tell God your fears and insecurities.

- Don't let harshness become a bad habit. Begin to replace it with gentleness one step at a time.

- Think before you speak. Do you really need to say what you're about to say?

- Spend time with a friend or family member with a gentle spirit. Let her gentleness rub off on you.

Whew! We've covered some ground in this chapter! Remember, this is not an exhaustive checklist of standards to try to meet. These are examples of attitudes that will turn your husband's heart toward you and toward God. These attitudes will grow and thrive only as you are being nourished by the Lord.

Many times as I was writing about a specific attitude, I had to stop writing as I was overwhelmed with feelings of "I don't want to show this attitude, I don't feel like showing this attitude, so how on earth can I write and tell other women to reflect these attitudes in their marriages?" I would stop my writing, wrestle with God about the attitude, finally come to a place of agreement with the Lord, and then sit back down at the keyboard. I know how challenging these attitudes can be! I constantly have to fight against doing marriage my way. However, I know that "there is a way which seems right to a man, but its end is the way of death" (Proverbs 14:12). I want to bring godly attitudes to my marriage, and I'm sure you do too, or you would not be reading this book.

PRAYER GUIDE

Heavenly Father,

Thank You, Lord, that You allow me to be a work in progress and that the Holy Spirit works in me to transform me. Thank You for never giving up on me. Thank You for never expecting me to be perfect or to earn Your love.

Help me show my husband the attitudes he needs in our marriage so that our marriage will glorify You. As I abide in You, Lord, I pray that I will bear fruit that makes me more like You. If I need to do something to guard my heart so I can develop the attitudes You desire, reveal that to me and make me willing to do whatever You ask of me. I ask these things in Your name. Amen.

7

Help for the Helper

Let's take a moment to pause and reflect on what we've learned so far. Are you seeing a transformation in your own life as you seek God? Are you seeing a transformation in your marriage as you apply God's truth to your marriage? I hope you are, and I hope you're encouraged to press on to know the Lord.

But perhaps you're not seeing the fruit of your labor. Perhaps you hoped for more changes in your husband and your marriage. I know those feelings.

But God reminds me that He is a God of relationships. He is with me every step of the way in my marriage journey. He is my Helper. In this chapter we'll look at some ways the Helper provides us with help along the journey of marriage.

A Helper Needs the Helper

Today the new puppy has proven quite a few times that she's not housebroken; one son is home with the stomach bug, so I'm missing a Bible study I really wanted to go to; my husband is out of town working, and before he left we had quite a fight; and…the day is not unfolding the way I'd planned!

On days like this we need to turn to the Lord our Helper, to the One who pours through us His love, strength, comfort, and contentment. Picture yourself dipping a cup into sparkling, clear spring water gushing from an opening in a rock in the side of a mountain. The water is shockingly cold, invigorating, and satisfying. Fill up the cup again and again, taking big, thirst-quenching gulps. Imagine this water replacing the stale, stagnant water you've been drinking.

Jesus invites us to come to Him: "He who believes in Me will never thirst" (John 6:35). "If anyone is thirsty, let him come to Me and drink…From his innermost being will flow rivers of living water" (John 7:37-38). We come to the Lord to quench our thirst, knowing He's all we need, and in our refreshment we also find what we need to nourish our marriage.

Throughout this book I've reminded you to seek God first, and I'll remind you of that again. If you focus on having a better marriage, it will elude you. This book is filled with ideas and suggestions you can put into practice, but the one answer to a better marriage is Jesus. Turn to the One who created marriage and who created you and your husband. Surrendering your marriage to Jesus will transform your own heart and, as a result, your marriage.

God wants us to depend on Him for everything we need in our marriages. He tells us to ask for what we need (Matthew 7:7). And when we don't even know what to pray, "the Spirit Himself intercedes for us with groanings too deep for words" (Romans 8:26). When we become believers, we receive the Holy Spirit, also called the Helper (John 14:16-17), who becomes a permanent resident in us and helps us in many ways. He's our Teacher, Revealer of truth, and Comforter.

Take a Break

Debbie is a woman who amazes me. She truly finds joy in being a wife and mother to three children. Her home is inviting (but not perfect!), and she's taught me much about homemaking just by her example. She serves at church in the youth ministry, and somehow she finds time to exercise. She rarely seems rushed or frenzied, and she usually can be seen wearing a calm smile. How does this real woman do it? I finally asked her one day and have benefited from her answer. She explained,

> A long time ago I realized two things that changed my life. First, I need rest, and second, I can't do it all. I can only do what God wants me to do. Anything else is a waste of time.
>
> Before this realization, I tried to do it all. If someone asked me to help in children's church, I said sure. If the women needed help with an event, I said yes. I volunteered at the kids' schools, I took my children to every event under the sun, and I averaged about five hours of sleep each night. I was a walking zombie! I snapped at my husband and my kids, and life was not fun.

Debbie first mentioned her need for rest. Are you rested? A helper to her husband needs rest! God made us as spiritual, emotional, *and* physical beings. He created us, and He created us to need rest. Some people need eight hours of sleep; some people need less. Some people could benefit from a nap; some people find that makes them groggy. One marriage counselor said that one of the first things he would ask a couple considering divorce would be how much sleep they get at night.

In addition to getting adequate sleep, you can find rest just by being still and quiet. Some women are addicted to busyness, and they're unsure of what they would do if they weren't doing something. Is that you? Debbie said she learned to do only what God wanted her to do. Ask yourself, *Have I prayed to see if this activity is what God wants me to do?* God will give you the time and energy you need to do His will. Even good things can keep us too busy and keep us from God's plan for us.

Some women fall into a martyr syndrome. They think they can't possibly rest because they have so much to do. Who's going to pay the bills, do the grocery shopping, take the kids to practices, cook the meals, and on and on unless they do? They think they have to do it all, won't ask anyone for help, and won't consider dropping things from their "things I *have* to do" list.

These women may seem sacrificial, but if you look a little deeper, they are often practicing false humility and being prideful. Maybe the real reason they don't ask for help is that they want others to think they can handle things on their own. Or maybe they want others to think they're incredibly wonderful for all they do and give. Or maybe they think no one else can do things right! You'll have to be honest with yourself to see if you fall into one of these categories, but please realize God made us to need Him and to need others. In marriage God clearly wants us to serve one another. Tell your husband what you need—not in a demanding way but in an honest way.

When you stop doing, you can just be. The best place to find rest is in the quiet with Jesus. Go to Him to exchange your worries for His peace, your questions for His assurance, and your tears for His comfort.

> I have learned something significant about laying my head on Jesus' shoulder. Jesus offers us not just mental rest from the noise and chaos of the world, not just physical rest from the work and demands, not just soul rest from our worries and problems, but a deep invigorating rest in Him. The deeper rest He describes is a transforming rest. When you and I come to Him, when we ask Him to become the Lord and Savior of our lives, He bestows on us a quiet rest not found anywhere else on earth. It is a peaceful rest that passes the world's understanding.[1]

Don't Forget to Have Some Fun!

"A joyful heart is good medicine, but a broken spirit dries up the bones" (Proverbs 17:22). What refreshes your soul? What restores joy in you? What's medicine for your broken spirit? Find it and enjoy it!

As a woman, I'm many things, only one of which is a wife. Ladies, taking a break from the many roles and responsibilities of your life is okay! And you can do this without feeling guilty! No, this is not permission to be selfish or to neglect your responsibilities. It's simply my observation that sometimes the best thing I can do for everyone else around me is to lighten my heart by having fun.

God created so much that is beautiful for us to enjoy. What delights me may be quite different from what tickles you. The key is to relish the moment, thank God for simple pleasures, and enjoy a fresh perspective. Here are a few ideas for fun: Go to a book store or library, take a bubble bath, go horseback riding, sit outside, plant flowers, get together with a friend, go for a walk or a bike ride, meet a friend for lunch at a favorite restaurant, take time to work on your scrapbook, play the piano, draw or paint or decorate, rent a funny movie and laugh hard, rent a sappy movie and shed a few tears, light candles and sit quietly, go to a coffee shop with a friend or by yourself, knit a scarf.

In some seasons of your life, your responsibilities may hinder you from finding time away from anything and anyone. You may get 15 minutes; other times you might get a few hours. You might get some time once a week or once per year. Make the most with the time you do get. Be wise and do something that truly refreshes you.

A Helper Needs Friends

"Behold, the bondslave of the Lord; may it be done to me according to your word" (Luke 1:38). This is Mary's response when the angel Gabriel appeared to her to tell her the incredible destiny she was to be a part of. Mary, an unmarried young virgin, heard an incredible story that she was pregnant by the Holy Spirit with God's child, Jesus. What a beautiful response of submission to God. What an incredible plan God blessed her with because of her willing acceptance and obedience!

One part of this story that just delights me is that she ran to tell her news to her cousin and friend Elizabeth. What a blessing Elizabeth's friendship was to Mary. Elizabeth herself was miraculously pregnant in her old age and had already accepted in faith that Mary was pregnant with the Son of God. These two friends shared each other's joy and supported one another in their journeys of faith.

I like to think about how God knew these two women would need each other. God knows what kind of friends we need and when. My friends are ones with whom I can laugh, cry, and share the joys and trials of life. We support one another when the road gets rough, and most importantly, we share the joy of walking hand in hand with each other and the Lord.

When I think back to the earlier years of raising children, I am thankful that God knew I needed a friend who would help me carry the load of raising children. Nancy lived in my neighborhood and had two sons almost the same ages as mine, and the four boys loved playing with each other. Nancy and I would hang out together, and we'd swap kids so we could both get some rest and refreshment. I am thankful that God provided just what I needed.

God gives us another picture of friendship in Exodus when the Israelites are fighting against the Amalekites. Moses went to the top of a hill and held up his arms as God instructed him to do. With him are Aaron and Hur. As long as Moses held up his hands, Israel prevailed, but when he lowered his hands, they fell back. "But Moses' hands were heavy. Then they took a stone and put it under him, and he sat on it; and Aaron and Hur supported his hands, one on one side and one on the other" (Exodus 17:12-13).

A woman needs her friends to hold her hands up as she seeks to be the kind of wife God wants her to be and her husband needs her to be. We need women friends who will lovingly hold us accountable to God's standards. "Iron sharpens iron, so one man sharpens another" (Proverbs 27:17). We need like-minded friends, friends who also seek to be godly wives.

I've learned so much from my friends about being a godly wife. Catherine has never, ever said a critical word about her husband to me, and she adapts to his busy schedule with gracious flexibility. Holly is careful to keep her spending within her budget, and if she's visiting at my house, she makes sure she leaves to have dinner ready for her husband's return from work. Amy bakes her husband's favorite treats, Lysa tidies up the house before her husband gets home, Ginny plays golf with her husband, Becky keeps the romantic fires burning, and Kelly offers me wise counsel and prays for my marriage. These are just a few ways the friends in my life have shown me that serving their husbands is a priority to them too. Their examples encourage me to look for ways to continue loving my husband.

What if you're reading this and you realize that you do not have the kind of friend who will support you in being a godly wife? First, ask God for one! Ask God specifically for what you need. You never know when or how He will answer that prayer, but keep your eyes open. Lisa, who is currently the teacher of a marriage Bible study I'm in, became my friend initially through an exchange of e-mails! Second, let God be your Friend. He loves you and cares about every detail of your life. He knows what you need. Third, ask yourself if you're being the kind of friend you'd like to have. Are you a friend who complains constantly about her husband, or are you sharing with others your heart's desire to let God change you and your marriage?

Make sure your friendships with women enhance your marriage. When I first got married, I remember my husband telling me he felt like an outsider when my twin sister and I were together. I didn't really understand what he meant until some years passed and my friendship with Scott became deeper and closer. I want Scott to be my closest friend, but I also know that women friends can refresh me with the understanding that can only come from another woman, someone who knows the details of being a wife and mother. I'm thankful for the good friends God has given me through the years, and at the same time I want to be careful that my husband never feels that my friends are more important than he is. My husband needs my friendship with him to be a priority.

One final word of warning, a warning which to some may sound extreme: If you're married, do not have close friendships with other men. Period. The end. You are playing with fire. You are fooling yourself if you think you can be close to another man without adversely affecting your marriage. I have heard of women and have personally known women who were in supposedly innocent friendships that did not stay innocent for very long. As a wife you honor God by reserving your emotional intimacy, and of course other forms of intimacy, for your husband. This is one way to honor the gift of marriage God has entrusted to you.

Stinkin' Thinkin'

> Watch your thoughts; they become words.
> Watch your words; they become actions.
> Watch your actions; they become habits.
> Watch your habits; they become character.
> Watch your character; it becomes your destiny.

Your thoughts become…your destiny. They shape you and mold you. *Wow!* This information about stinkin' thinkin' has transformed all areas of my life more than anything else I've learned in recent years. Are you getting the message? Pay attention! Read slowly and with a prayerful heart. Put on your listening ears and pray that the eyes of your heart may be enlightened. Please pray the following prayer before you continue reading.

> *Dear Father, You are truth, and I pray that this truth we are about to discuss will penetrate deeply. I pray that You will bind Satan right now. He is a liar and a deceiver, and I want nothing to do with him. I want to hear Your truth and apply it to my life. I come to You in Jesus' name. Amen.*

So what's so important that I've spent a paragraph warning you to pay attention? Our thoughts determine our actions. Let me say it again. Our thoughts determine our actions.

Mark sat at his computer in his den, a place he spent quite a bit of time. He paid most of his bills on-line, but he also had games on his computer to distract him and the Internet tempting him. He'd looked at some "racy" sights, but what was wrong with that? He hadn't crossed over the line to real pornography. And besides, his wife was never interested in having sex. What was a guy supposed to do? He could hear the kids arguing in the other room, so he stomped out of the room and yelled at them to shut up or else. He sat back down in his den, turned on the TV, and was in his own world. He hoped Sandra didn't come in and bother him about something she wanted him to do.

Meanwhile, Sandra was cleaning up the kitchen after their Sunday lunch. This was their routine: Go to church, eat the big lunch she'd prepared, and she'd clean up while Mark hid in his den. Wasn't that just typical? He was leaving her with all the work, as usual. And what did he do on Sundays? Just about whatever he wanted to do. So much for doing something fun with the whole family. They hardly had a conversation anymore. At least he could have helped her with some of the chores. He helped only when she got mad and yelled at him. Sometimes he'd finally get involved, but more often than not they just ended up having a big fight, and he'd stomp off to his den. Some things never change...

This scenario resonates with me, not because my marriage was specifically like this but because this couple is stuck and they don't know how to get out of this rut. Their stinkin' thinkin' has left them hopeless that their marriage can change. I know how that feels. As I explained in the beginning of this book, my marriage started to change when I took a good look at myself and an eye-opening look at God's Word.

Understanding that my thoughts determine my actions was an epiphany for me, one of those "aha" moments. Now that I've lived and walked this truth, it all seems so obvious, but marriage is a battlefield, and Satan had done a good job of deceiving me for many years. I had listened to Satan's lies before I got married, and I carried a heap of lies into my marriage.

Joyce Meyer's book *Battlefield of the Mind* was so instrumental in opening my eyes to the impact of my thoughts. She explains Satan's strategy:

He begins by bombarding our mind with cleverly
devised patterns of little nagging thoughts, suspicions,

doubts, fears, wonderings, reasonings and theories. He moves slowly and cautiously (after all, well-laid plans take time). Remember, he has a strategy for his warfare. He has studied us for a long time. He knows what we like and what we don't like. He knows our insecurities, our weaknesses and our fears. He knows what bothers us most. He is willing to invest any amount of time it takes to defeat us. One of the devil's strong points is patience.[2]

Marriage is a battlefield. If God is for something, the enemy, Satan, is against it. Just as he did in the Garden of Eden, Satan distorts God's Word, offers up lies, and waits to see what we'll do with them. If we buy into his lies, we're one step closer to the destruction of our marriage.

Satan gets a lot of bang for his buck when he attacks marriage. If one marriage suffers, the future marriages of the children witnessing the strife may also suffer, as might the marriages of other family members and friends who are witnessing this crumbling relationship. If Satan can destroy a marriage, he can throw in some other damage along with it. A failing marriage is like a drowning man latching on to someone else to prevent himself from drowning—he takes others down with him.

But wait! Satan is not stronger than God; he is not omniscient and omnipotent like God. The drowning man can cling to the One who has the strength to rescue him, Jesus Christ. "The thief comes only to steal and kill and destroy; I came that they may have life, and have it abundantly" (John 10:10). Jesus will not allow Satan to steal the abundant life He has promised us, but we have to take action against Satan.

God has given us a powerful strategy to defeat Satan.

- Recognize you have "the mind of Christ" (1 Corinthians 2:16).

- "Examine everything carefully; hold fast to that which is good" (1 Thessalonians 5:21).

- Take "every thought captive to the obedience of Christ" (2 Corinthians 10:5).

The Mind of Christ

The day you become a Christian, you receive the Holy Spirit, who gives you Christ's mind-set. You can look at life from Christ's perspective right now. So what does this have to do with marriage? Ask yourself, *Is what I'm thinking about my husband and my marriage something that Jesus would think?* If not, then it's a thought you need to get rid of! You can pray to have God's perspective on your marriage. Ask Him to help you see your husband the way He does. Scripture says that "the mind set on the Spirit is life and peace" (Romans 8:6). To make progress in your marriage you have to become very intentional about where you set your thoughts. You have to replace your stinkin' thinkin' with God's truth.

Examine Everything Carefully

Examine your thoughts. Become aware of your stinkin' thinkin'. Let's revisit Mark and Sandra. What are their thoughts set on? Mark is set on escaping, so he probably has thoughts like these: *My marriage is a hassle and aggravation. Sandra doesn't understand me, so I'm not going to bother talking to her. She's bossy, critical, and controlling. She's not meeting my sexual needs, so I have the right to get them met through another means.*

Sandra is angry most of the time. Let's look at Sandra's thoughts: *Mark doesn't do a thing in this family. If I don't do it, it won't get done. He's checked out. That's just fine. I can check out too. I won't talk to him unless I absolutely have to.*

Mark and Sandra have repeated these negative thoughts for so long that these lies have become fortresses or strongholds in their marriage. The dictionary says a stronghold is "an area distinguished by a certain quality." Repetition develops strongholds in our minds. What strongholds have developed in your mind about your marriage? Pray right now for God to reveal Satan's lies to you.

As I prayed this for my own marriage, I began to clearly see how much of the world's messages I'd adopted into my own thinking. I've been a Christian since I was 16 years old, but for a long time instead of asking what God wanted me to think, I just adopted other people's views. This process was very subtle, as Satan often is.

Let me give you an example. I grew up in a feminist era, and I believe the negative aspects of feminism affect many marriages today. Specifically I began to see how much male bashing I'd been exposed to by the people in my life, the books I read, and the TV shows I watched. Women often feel as if they have to prove they're as good as men, often by ridiculing or showing contempt for men.

Male-bashing opinions include these: Men just want women to stay in the kitchen, men think they're superior to women, men wouldn't be anywhere without women, and men need to recognize that women are equal to men in all ways. Often in my marriage I would brandish these thoughts like a sword to protect myself from getting hurt. Of course, my marriage was ultimately the victim of this warfare.

Over the past few years I have become aware of what I'm thinking. I'm also becoming more aware of what affects my thought patterns. God has asked me to get radical about what I'm putting into my thoughts. "If your eye causes you to stumble, pluck it out and throw it from you. It is better for you to enter life with one eye, than to have two eyes and be cast into the fiery hell" (Matthew 18:9). Now that's radical! I am more careful about the TV shows and movies I watch, the books I read, and the company I keep. Is your thought life an area you need to get radical about for the sake of your marriage? An area you need to guard? God will reveal this to you.

Take Every Thought Captive to the Obedience of Christ

Our strategy to defeat Satan is to acknowledge that as Christians we have the mind of Christ. Then we must examine our thoughts to become aware of any that are not aligned with God's. Finally, we can take every thought captive to the obedience of Christ.

Let's look at some marriage situations and see how to take every thought captive to Christ. How would you respond in these situations?

Scenario One

Your husband just spent almost $1500 on a new John Deere even though he recently told you that now wasn't the best time to buy new furniture. How do you respond?

Old thoughts: I can't believe how selfish he is! He's always thinking about himself! I'll show him. I'll just go charge the new couch I've been wanting.

New thoughts: Well, that will be a big help to him and will give him more time with the family. He works so hard and has so little free time at home. This riding lawn mower will save him a lot of time. Lord, help me to have an attitude that blesses him and his decision to make this purchase. Give me contentment and help me not to seek getting my own way. Give me the right time to talk to my husband about future purchases.

Scenario Two

You've got a great dinner ready for your family. Your husband told you he'd be home at 6:00 PM. He calls at 6:15 to tell you he's running late, so he's going to have to grab a quick sandwich, change into his softball clothes, and rush to the game starting at 7:00 PM. Softball game? What softball game?

Old thoughts: I am so sick of cooking dinners that he never even eats. And *once again* he didn't talk with me about his schedule. I had no idea about the softball game. Great, I'll be home alone cleaning up the kitchen and putting the kids to bed—same old, same old. I think I'll just make plans for one night this week and "forget" to tell him about them.

New thoughts: I'm mad, and I want to lash out at him. Lord, help me be patient and not provoked. Give us a time later when I'm not feeling so angry to let him know how I feel when he neglects to communicate his schedule to me. Help me to do it in a respectful and loving manner, knowing that I have areas I need to work on too.

To take every thought captive to Christ means to become aware of the lies you're repeating to yourself. Next you choose not to believe the lies or to harbor them in your thoughts. Then speak truth to yourself!

You can do this! Call on the Lord in the heat of the battle! The battles may be hard, but you will win!

Although I was a girlie-girl when I was younger, I actually did go deep-sea fishing in south Florida a time or two. I remember sometimes the fishing was so easy that we'd get into a school of fish and couldn't catch them fast enough. We'd quickly put a little bait on a hook and line without even using a fishing rod, throw the line overboard, and pull in a fish. We'd do this over and over until we were completely exhausted. Other times, however, we would get worn out wrestling a particular stubborn and combative fish. Sometimes we'd win and pull that fish into the boat, but other times the line would snap, and the fish would be gone.

Keep this picture in your mind as you think about taking your thoughts captive to Christ. Just like the fish, some thoughts will be caught easily, while others will require all your efforts—especially thoughts that have become strongholds. You've probably spent many years developing certain strongholds in your mind, and Satan will fight for you to keep those negative thoughts. Keep fighting back! Stand firm with God, and you will be victorious! Replace the lies with God's Word.

We've been talking in this book about God transforming us to be what He wants us to be and what our husbands need us to be. That transformation begins in the mind. "And do not be conformed to this world, but be transformed by the renewing of your mind, so that you may prove what the will of God is, that which is good and acceptable and perfect" (Romans 12:2). Become aware of your thoughts and choose to line them up with the mind of Christ. Take your thoughts captive before you become bitter, unforgiving, resentful, angry, or hopeless. Your marriage will be transformed!

God Is Faithful

Yesterday by about 7:00 PM I was just plain tired. I get up early each morning to write before the kids wake up because that seems to be the most creative and productive writing time for me. So by the evening hour I'm running out of steam. However, after dinner I still have numerous tasks to finish. The kitchen needs to be cleaned, kids need to finish homework and get their backpacks ready for the next day, phone calls need returning, writing needs to be finished, little boys and puppies need tending to. Some days I wonder how I can finish the tasks before me, and honestly some days I do not handle this time gracefully.

Yesterday, all I could think was *I'm tired and I need help.* My usual tendency is to try to dump the whole load of responsibilities on Scott if he's around! But this time I stopped myself, and I took my thoughts captive, filling my mind with God's Word. *Lord, You promise that You will be my portion, that You will make me strong and let my heart take courage as I hope in You. Lord, be the strength I need right now.*

And right at that moment, while I was at the kitchen sink doing dishes, God filled me with peace, strength, and the ability to press on in a cheerful frame of mind. God was there just when I needed Him. "Faithful is He who calls you, and He also will bring it to pass" (1 Thessalonians 5:24).

PRAYER GUIDE

Dear Lord,

When I am thirsty, I pray that You alone will quench my thirst. Let nothing else satisfy me. I want to be a woman who depends on You, Lord. Thank You that the Holy Spirit lives in me, teaching me, helping me, and strengthening me. Thank You for the gifts of my husband and children. Sometimes, Lord, I feel overwhelmed with the responsibilities of my life. At those times, Lord, show me how to adopt Your priorities for my life. Help me to give my gifts and energy only to what You call me to.

Provide for me refreshing alone time with You, Lord, and time to enjoy the good things You've given me to enjoy. Thank You for laughter, and thank You for friends who love You and encourage me to love You. Show me any lies I'm believing about my husband or my marriage. Lead me to the truth You want me to replace the lies with. I ask these thing in Your name. Amen.

8

Hearts at Home

⁓

Suzie had been on the phone with her mother for half an hour. Her two oldest sons were fighting over a toy, and her youngest son was clinging to her leg while crying for her attention. A talk show blared from the television in the family room while a cartoon character shrieked from the TV upstairs.

"Mom, hang on. These kids are making me crazy." As she took a breath from her phone conversation, she hollered at Luke to go play and threatened the two older boys by reminding them their father would be home soon and would take care of them.

Into this bedlam walked her husband, Jim, his weariness from the long day compounded by the chaotic scene greeting him.

"What's for dinner?" asked Jim, with fear and trembling in his voice. With a sigh of exasperation, Suzie put the phone up to her ear and told her mom to keep holding on.

"Cereal, unless you want to go to the store and get something, and if you do, get something for the kids too. I just haven't had time to make dinner."

I can assure you that on many nights, the scene my husband walks into is not as peaceful as I'd like it to be. I hope Suzie's story causes you to think about the atmosphere of your home, for the wife truly is the heart of the home. Suzie's attitude and actions scream to her husband, "You are not important!"

In previous chapters we looked at attitudes that a husband needs his wife to exhibit. In this chapter we'll see how our homes can reflect our loving hearts. We'll look specifically at a wife's roles as a homemaker and a mother. As we consider these two areas, let's give God our hearts so that He can take them in His loving hands and mold them until they reflect His own. "The king's heart is like channels of water in the hand of the LORD; He turns it wherever He wishes" (Proverbs 21:1).

What Is a Homemaker?

Let's look once again at Paul's letter to Titus to understand what God says about wives as homemakers.

> Older women likewise are to be reverent in their behavior, not malicious gossips nor enslaved to much wine, teaching what is good, so that they may encourage the young women to love their husbands, to love their children, to be sensible, pure, workers at home, kind, being subject to their own husbands, so that the word of God will not be dishonored (Titus 2:3-5).

This Scripture tells us that women are to be "workers at home." Proverbs 31:10-31 also spells out some of the responsibilities of a worker at home. Of these 22 verses in Proverbs, half refer to homemaking tasks.

Now, don't go running scared! The word *homemaker* sets some of us modern women on edge! We're frightened by visions of unending laundry, scrubbed floors that never stay clean, countless meals and cleanups, and a woman who is expected to do all the housework by herself. Well, let's remember that a wife is many things, only one of which is a homemaker. She is a beloved child of God, a helper to her husband, and a uniquely created female, to name a few. However, we cannot escape noticing that part of her role as a wife is to be a worker at home. Whether or not you have a job outside the home, you are to be a homemaker.

The Heart of Homemaking

We will discuss some practical aspects of keeping a home, but first let's look at the heart of a homemaker. Before we find a list of specific activities for wives in Proverbs 31, we read this: "An excellent wife, who can find? For her worth is far above jewels. The heart of her husband trusts in her, and he will have no lack of gain. She does him good and not evil all the days of her life" (Proverbs 31:10-11). First, note that according to God, being a wife is a worthy and valuable role. Do you believe that? Do you believe that being a wife is a worthy calling? God says it is!

Next, notice what is said about the husband of an excellent wife—he trusts her. Let's remember that all the wife's activities should lead her husband to say that he trusts her, that he can count on her to enhance his life. I want my husband to feel his life is better having been married to me. Last, we bring honor to God when we fulfill this role (Titus 2:5). In this respect my homemaking is a reflection of my relationship with Christ and my willingness to be obedient in this area.

When I think about being a homemaker, the most important question to me is, what climate do I want in my home? Since this book is about what our husbands need, let's also ask, what climate does my husband want in our home? Many husbands may not even be able to articulate what they want. Maybe they can say what they don't want— they don't want chaos and conflict. It's safe to say that most men want peace and refuge. They want their homes to be places where they can recharge their batteries.

I am the one who is responsible for creating that climate in our home, the one who turns a house into a home by bringing feminine touches of beauty and creativity. My family values a climate of order, peace, comfort, love, and fun. I've learned to value this climate over 15 years of marriage as I've observed what ministers to my husband and family. Ask God what climate He wants you to create in your home, and then ask Him to help you create that atmosphere.

Let's look at some practical aspects of homemaking. I'll share some guidelines that have helped me.

Be at Home

A homemaker needs to be at home. Sounds obvious, but this can be a challenge! Last year Zachary was in fourth grade, and Tyler was in kindergarten—both of my sons were in school full-time for the first time. I spread my wings all over Charlotte for quite a few months. I got together with friends, shopped, and went to Bible studies. Gradually God helped me see that my flitting about needed to come to an end. Right now I know He wants me at home more, studying His Word, writing, and being a homemaker.

Being a homemaker starts by looking at your schedule and managing your time. Are you home? You have to be! Even good things, such as ministry at church, can take you away from the best thing, ministry at home. You will have to say no to some things, realizing you are accountable to God for your home. Some people may not understand when you say no, but if you set your eyes on your Audience of One, what others think or say will matter less and less to you.

Marybeth Whalen, author, speaker for Proverbs 31 Ministries, and mother of six children, embraces her calling as a homemaker, but that hasn't always been true.

> When my first child was born, I can remember looking at my calendar each week and being disappointed if we did not have somewhere to be each day. The days I had to be home were depressing to me, and I thought of my house as a prison. When my little boy began to talk, I can remember him waking up in the morning, putting his two little feet on the floor, and looking at me expectantly. "Go?" he would ask. He knew we were bound to be going somewhere.
>
> However, the birth of more children and the logistics of

getting out made "going" more complicated. Soon, God had my attention as He lovingly turned my attention back to the place I was trying to avoid. I met other women who helped to foster a love for creating a true home—one unlike anything I had ever had as a child growing up in a single-parent household. As I began to create a warm, inviting, clean home for my family, I began to want to be there more. Instead of being a prison, it became a magnet, drawing all of us into its warmth. I was proud of this haven I had made, with God's help, for my family. I continue to learn about homemaking and all that it entails, and I love the days on my calendar now that don't involve going, so I can rest, work, and enjoy being home.

Sometimes we can feel like captives in our homes. When I feel this way, I ask God to change my perspective and let it mirror His eternal one. I thank God for as many specific blessings as I can think of. God then reminds me that as a homemaker I am in a privileged position to care for what God has blessed me with. I am able to work as a writer from home now, but for many years I worked as a full-time high school English teacher. During those years I longed to stay at home. So now on days when I feel less than motivated, I can remember that God has blessed me with this position. In fact, this is the very place I prayed to be! Sometimes we forget to be thankful for our answered prayers, don't we?

Staying home requires you to manage your schedule carefully. Many women I know manage to do all their errands on one day. They devote the other days to being at home.

Many aspects of being a homemaker can be challenging, so find ways to motivate yourself. I often cling to the promise of 1 Thessalonians 5:24, which promises that if God calls me to do something, He'll make me able to do it: "Faithful is He who calls you, and He also will bring it to pass." For extra motivation, post verses around your house to remind you of God's truth. This one would be a good one to keep visible.

Avoid Idleness

Tyler recently started responding in an endearing way when I ask him to do something. His new response is "I'm on it!" The Proverbs 31 woman is "on it!" The list of her activities in Proverbs 31 is exhausting! Of course, she doesn't do all these things in one day, but Scripture makes clear that she does not waste time. "She looks well to the way of her household, and does not eat the bread of idleness" (Proverbs 31:27). Synonyms for *idle* are *lazy, shiftless,* and *without purpose.* I don't want to be those things! What can tempt us toward idleness? Watching TV, time on the computer, reading, and talking on the phone are a few things that come to my mind. Nothing is inherently wrong with any of these activities, but there's a proper time for everything.

My mother is a great role model for avoiding idleness. She's tireless! Even today she can wear me out with energy! I remember that when I was growing up she just kept moving. Sometimes we have to tell ourselves to just keep moving. Play music, pray while you're working in the house, and look forward to that great feeling at the end of getting tasks accomplished.

Study Homemaking

Learn from others. My mother is an accomplished cook, housekeeper, and time manager. I wasn't too keen on learning from her when I was a stubborn and rebellious teenager, but in later years I've valued the example she set. On that note, remember that you are a model to your own children. What example as a homemaker are you giving them?

I learn much from my friends. Kelly has a gift of decorating in a way that makes her home welcoming and inviting. Karen knows the art of finding incredible bargains. Amy's a fantastic cook. Rita is amazingly efficient at cleaning her house. What can you learn from your friends? Don't be shy about asking for their help!

Talk to your friends and read books or Internet articles on homemaking. Just make sure you actually put into action the ideas you gather! Check out www.FlyLady.net. This website offers encouraging and manageable household tips. One of FlyLady's tips is to set the timer for 15 minutes and do what you can during that time. I love the simplicity of that task.

Managing the Home

Someone has to manage the "stuff" of life, including the house, cars, yard, furniture, toys, clothes, paperwork, finances, and pets. If you own material things, someone has to take care of them! God says you as a wife are the caretaker of your home. You're not just the housekeeper or gardener; you're a manager.

As a manager you do not do everything yourself. You and your family work together to decide who does what. As you develop routines, they'll soon become habits that will help you stay on top of home management.

The Proverbs 31 woman "smiles at the future" (Proverbs 31:25) because she has an overall plan for her homemaking. She "looks well to the ways of her household" (Proverbs 31:27). She's ready at the right time with the right thing her family needs. This tells me that much of being a homemaker is looking ahead and being prepared. Using the acronym PREPARED, here are some practical tips for being a homemaker.

*P*ray at the start of each day for God's agenda and priorities to be on display in your home. How can you best minister to your husband and children? I like to have a plan, but I also want to be flexible for the unplanned moments, such as when friends stop by or my son wants me to sit and watch him shoot baskets. I never want to make loved ones, especially my husband, feel like an interruption.

*R*eady yourself for what comes next. Being ready or prepared for the future is a trademark of the Proverbs 31 woman. She "rises also while it is still night" (Proverbs 31:15) and "her lamp does not go out at night" (Proverbs 31:18). "She is not afraid of the snow" (Proverbs 31:21) because she has her winter clothing ready. Readiness is evident in our households when we have a budget and plan expenditures accordingly, when we periodically go through the children's clothes to get ready for the next season, when we have plenty of paper towels and toilet paper on hand, when we've grocery shopped following a planned menu of healthy meals, when the children have school supplies they need, and when our work clothes are clean and ironed the night before.

*E*xercise and eat good foods that give you energy. I must be honest and tell you that of all these tips, this is the most challenging for me! I know that if I take even 20 minutes per day to walk or do an exercise video I'll feel so much better and have more energy for the day. I also know that eating too much sugar or drinking too much caffeine sets me on edge, making me irritable and less patient. Taking care of myself physically is not just for me; it's for my family too.

*P*lan your household chores. Have a plan that suits you. I like to clean the entire house in one day simply because I savor the reward of a completely clean house. Then during the week I can spend a small amount of time each day keeping things fairly clean and in order. Other women like to do one major chore each day.

I've always followed one rule of thumb: Before I go to bed, I get ready for the next day. The kitchen is clean, the toys are picked up, and backpacks and lunches are ready for the next day. Again, find what suits you. "Household cleaning is only hard if you don't do it. It's really not that bad if you keep up with it and you kind of have a strategy and a plan of attack."[1]

A few years ago Scott purchased a Day Runner magnetic calendar, which has changed our lives! It's on the refrigerator where everyone can see it, and all activities go on this calendar. Another thing on my refrigerator is a magnetic notepad for a running grocery list. Anyone who thinks of something we need puts it on the list.

*A*rrange your home with order and organization in mind. Bins and baskets keep me sane. Bins are great for children's toys. Kids learn from an early age to pick things up and put toys in their proper place.

Baskets were the answer for me and Scott early in our marriage. You know how certain things just push your buttons? Well, one of my buttons is pushed when Scott dumps stuff on the kitchen countertops.

Early in our marriage we decided we'd each have a basket or a drawer for "dumping" stuff. Scott puts everything from his pockets—wallet, keys, loose change, cell phone, (thank goodness women have purses)—in his basket. Or if he doesn't and I want to tidy up, I put it in the basket. Then he knows where it is, and the kitchen counters are clear. If you have enough drawers, assigning a drawer to each family member works the same way.

*R*id yourself of unused items. I find it very cathartic to get rid of things! About every two months I make a Goodwill bag and a throwaway bag. I look at things like my clothes, the kids' clothes and toys, and files, and I ask myself if we've used these things in the past year. If it's something of my husband's, I put it aside for him to look at later.

*E*xamine your purchases. My friend Chere has always been careful about accumulating stuff because she's married to a pilot, and their family has moved frequently. She pointed out one day when we were shopping that the more things she owns, the more things she has to take care of. Good point!

*D*elight yourself in the Lord. He is the strength you need to carry out His plan for you. "The joy of the LORD is your strength" (Nehemiah 8:10).

But I Just Don't Want To!

Being a homemaker is more than just doing household chores, but it's easy to get bogged down in them. Several things can make homemaking a challenge. First, I can easily be tempted to believe that what I'm doing isn't as valuable as earning a paycheck. When that thought comes to mind, I just need to go back to God's Word. An excellent wife's "worth is far above jewels" (Proverbs 31:10). I must have God's perspective, not the world's. Second, the chores never end! As soon as you get all the laundry finished, someone adds something dirty to the clothes hamper. That's just life. I'm sure my husband has that same thought when he gets up at 5:00 AM to go to work. Third, I may never get thanks from my husband or children for all the things I do, but they're likely to notice when I haven't done them. My motive has to be to please and honor God. Sometimes I have to tell myself, *God sees, God sees, God sees.*

Serving Your Husband in Love

I was staying for a weekend with my newly married friend Shannon and her husband, Tom. At about 9:00 PM, we were all lounging around, watching TV, and feeling very relaxed. Tom mentioned he would love some chocolate chip cookies. Shannon said they didn't have any, but she would make some. And that's just what she did! From scratch, no less! Fourteen years later, that memory is still with me. I was absolutely astounded that Shannon did that. Tom had not asked her to make cookies. We were all comfortable and sleepy from a big meal. I know I didn't feel like moving, and she probably didn't either. But Shannon wasn't thinking about herself. She had a servant's heart and wanted to make her husband happy.

So as a homemaker, I ask myself, *What's important to my husband, me, and my children? How can my home bring glory to God?* You can observe your husband's preferences, you can ask him, and you can pray for God to show you.

Little things make my husband feel loved. Scott travels, and often when he gets back home, he's tired of heavy restaurant meals and just wants a bowl of cereal. Making sure I have milk and his favorite cereal lets him know I'm thinking of him. Scott has never, ever asked me to iron anything for him, but he needs an ironed shirt for work every day, so that's another little thing I can do to serve him. Also, Scott has the gift of hospitality. He loves to invite people over, sometimes spontaneously, so I want to have the home fairly ready for friends.

Homemaking is not about having a perfectly clean house or expensive furnishings. If those are my most important goals, then my home has become an idol. Homemaking is about embracing the most important people in my life—my family—with love. I am so thankful that home is our favorite place to be, and I pray it always will be.

I've always loved Amy Grant's "If These Walls Could Speak" because it makes me think about the memories I'm creating in my home. What memories do you want your home to hold? Home is a place where we laugh and giggle as Scott does the Daddy Dance, where I teach my sons how to make a birthday cake (okay, from a box!), where we have family movie night, where my husband and I snuggle on the couch, where we pray together, and where we gather around the dinner table with good friends. Home is a place where I'll remember wiping tears, reading favorite books and the Bible together, hugging tighter than tight, singing "Amazing Grace" to Zachary when he was little, decorating the Christmas tree, playing Uno and Boggle, shooting nerf baskets, and watching the Minnesota Vikings on TV.

What memories do your walls hold or do you want them to hold in the future? May our homemaking always be one way to love our husbands and to create memories our families will treasure for years.

Cherishing Children

"By wisdom a house is built, and by understanding it is established; and by knowledge the rooms are filled with all precious and pleasant riches" (Proverbs 24:3-4). The greatest riches in any home are the family members. God tells us that "children are a gift of the LORD" (Psalm 127:3). God wants us to love our children with the kind of *agape* love 1 Corinthians 13 describes and with an affectionate love that treasures our children.

Since I consider myself a girlie-girl, I always imagined that one day I'd be the mother of a little girl to whom I could pass down my Barbies, share the love of pink, and teach the fine art of shopping for clothes. However, God had a different plan, as I am now the mother of two boys who play every kind of sport, have Legos spread out in every inch of the house, and convinced me to keep a basketball hoop in the dining room. Despite this not being quite what I imagined, I love being a mother and have embraced this role in my life.

A husband needs his wife to be content as a mother. Can you say that about yourself? Do you cherish your role as a mother? Does your husband hear more about the problems with the kids or more about your love for them? Do your children know they're among your top priorities? Do they feel your love in the hugs, snuggles, and joy you show when you're with them? Do they see your love when you listen to their stories? Do they hear your gentle "I love you" at the end of each day? Or do your kids hear from you critical and impatient words with a harsh tone of voice? Are you constantly trying to get away from your kids by scheduling way too many activities? Do you let the TV and game systems do the babysitting? Do they sense that you'd rather be doing anything else but being a mother?

As much as I love motherhood, I'm the first to admit that being a mother, like anything else, can feel like the best of times or the worst of times. When your little boy spontaneously hugs you and says he loves you the most, you feel like being a mother is the greatest calling ever. But when your preteen daughter acts sassy and unappreciative, you might wonder why you're trying so hard.

Remember that God is a parent too. Throughout Scripture, God is called our Father. Matthew 6:6-11 reminds us that our Father sees everything, knows what we need before we ask Him, and provides our daily bread. What comforting reassurances for earthly parents from our heavenly Father.

Another help in parenting is a supportive friend. My friend Catherine understands the challenges of motherhood but also rejoices in the calling. When my children were younger, I was so thankful she had traveled farther down the road in her journey of motherhood. She reminded me then and still reminds me today that we have seasons for everything in motherhood—seasons when we feel elated and seasons of discouragement, seasons when we see the fruit of our labor and seasons when we wonder if our children learned anything good from us, seasons when we're exhausted and seasons when we soar.

I've learned so much from Catherine just by watching her live out her daily priorities of loving God, her husband, and her children. I'll always marvel at her joy and contentment in being a wife and mother. She enjoys being with her husband and three children more than anyone else in the world. She lights up when they enter the room. She gets off the phone with me if one of them has just arrived. She's prayed with them and for them for 25 years. These are just a few examples of her gift to me as a mentor. But most importantly, Catherine has truly modeled how to treasure her family members.

Treasuring our family means they get our best.

> Are my creativity, my wit, and my best efforts spent outside my family? Do they get only the leftovers? A sentence from Psalm 101 has been both challenging and convicting for me: "I will walk in my house with blameless heart" (Psalm 101:2). When God speaks to me about being more loving, this verse reminds me to make application in my family first—and then to others. It forces me to ask, "Am I more spiritual, more loving, or more fun some where else? Who gets my best—my family or others?"[2]

Another friend, Karen, reminds me to laugh and enjoy the journey of motherhood. In fact she has turned her wit and wisdom into a career and is now a humor columnist and author of the book *Invisible Underwear, Bus Stop Mommies, and Other Things True To Life.* She helps me and mothers across the nation laugh at the common threads of motherhood.

> Unfortunately, I wasted years of potential domestic bliss worrying about being productive. My husband came home every two weeks with a paycheck that proved he'd been productive every day. I stood there with snot shimmering on my shirt, a whiny kid on my hip and another running through the house naked except for the Desitin smeared over every inch of her body.
>
> Blame it on the feminist movement of the 60's and 70's. Blame it on my college degree. Whatever the reasons, I felt as a stay at home mother, I had to prove myself. I needed to produce tangible evidence of my productivity during "all that free time" at home. I was stupid.
>
> A productive mother is one who, at the end of the day, typically knows her children's names by the third try. She might even remember her own name and address.
>
> By the end of the day, the children of a productive mother will have eaten something; even if it was defrosted ten minutes

before mealtime. They most likely will have used a toothbrush, on their teeth, at least once. They're clean enough that even the dog will lick them. Their bathrooms are cleaner than those found at a rest area.

Every member of the household has enough underwear or diapers for one more day. Then again, even the most productive mother occasionally turns off her mind-reading capabilities and is informed by a resident teenager at 6:00 AM that his underwear drawer is empty. This is why baby powder was invented.

When our kids were still babies, my friend Beth called and shared with complete ease, "Sarah was sick yesterday and the only thing that made her happy was to be held and rocked. So that's what we did all day." I remember wishing I could sit and rock my baby boy without worrying about what wasn't getting done.

Yesterday, I brought my teenage boy home from the hospital following surgery. I pumped him full of pain medicine and got him settled on the couch. I pulled over the rocking chair, sat down and watched him sleep for hours.

It was a very productive day.[3]

A United Front

What's important in marriage when raising children? What does your husband need from you as a mother to your children?

One vital element to parenting that your husband needs from you is help in presenting a united front. This agreement in parenting reveals itself in so many ways. First, don't ever, ever take sides with your children if it means going against your husband. I've made this mistake, and as soon as I've done it, I've regretted it. It upset my husband, but it also distressed my children. Most children do not want to see their parents fight, for children get much of their security from the security of their parents' marriage. If you do disagree with your husband, can you support him in the moment and discuss the situation with him in private later? Your children are watching, and they'll see your desire to respect your husband.

You and your husband are a child-raising team. You show teamwork when you are in accord and when you share responsibilities. I know that some women feel as if they do everything with little or no help around the house and with the children. This was clearly never God's plan. So how do you approach a husband who you feel is not doing his part while still showing him love, submission, and respect? Prayerfully! Pour out your heart to God, share with Him your frustrations, and ask Him specifically for direction. Ask Him if you can talk to your husband about your frustrations. He promises to lead and guide you on the right path. Unfortunately, many women just stay frustrated without going to God in prayer.

If God does give you a green light for talking to your husband, ask God to give you the right timing and the right words (along with the right tone of voice and facial expression!). Ask your husband to let you know when a good time to talk would be.

Be careful, though, not to expect your husband to do things your way or the way a mother does them. Mothers and fathers can be united in purpose but different in approaches. Your children will be blessed by both a mother's input and a father's.

Parenting Priorities

Finally, be parents who are united in purpose. Have you as a couple decided what your priorities are for parenting? If you and your husband have never discussed your joint priorities for your children, now might be a great time to do that. One of the best ways you can support your husband is to support his priorities for your children. Ask your husband what his priorities are, write them down, and make it a point to honor them.

Even if your husband isn't interested in discussing parenting, you can always observe what's important to him. Does he value good manners in your children? Then make teaching manners a priority. Are there certain chores your husband wants the kids to do? Then make sure they complete their chores.

Some of our own parenting priorities have emerged just in the daily course of being parents. In other words, we didn't necessarily articulate them; we just did what we thought was best for our family.

For example, Scott grew up playing every kind of sport. So when

Zachary turned four, he was playing T-ball at the local YMCA. I did not grow up playing sports, but I certainly agree that trying out many things in life, sports included, is important.

Then a second son came along, life got busier, and I got frustrated sometimes at how much time our family dedicated to sports. Scott and I eventually defined our limits in this area. We agreed that one activity per season is the rule of thumb. We also agreed that other pursuits, such as church activities, art, and reading also need to be priorities. Other areas of our parenting have been more purposefully planned.

I'll share with you a few of the main priorities for our family. As you read these, consider what God wants as top priorities for your children.

We Teach Our Children to Love God

> Hear, O Israel! The LORD is our God, the LORD is one! You shall love the LORD your God with all your heart and with all your soul and with all your might. These words, which I am commanding you today, shall be on your heart. You shall teach them diligently to your sons and shall talk of them when you sit in your house and when you walk by the way and when you lie down and when you rise up. You shall bind them as a sign on your hand and they shall be as frontals on your forehead. You shall write them on the doorposts of your house and on your gates (Deuteronomy 6:4-9).

Our first priority as parents is to talk about God and to teach our children God's ways. God wants to be a part of our everyday lives, not just a God we know at church or Sunday school. God wants us in a Bible-based church, and He wants our children there too, so that's a starting point. However, we are not to leave the training to the church. Our number one job as parents is to point our children to Jesus Christ and to share with them that Jesus loves them, died to pay the price for their sins, and rose again to eternal life. We are to teach them through our words and example how to be followers of Christ. "Train up a child in the way he should go, even when he is old he will not depart from it" (Proverbs 22:6).

Training takes place in so many ways and places. The car is a great place for telling a Bible story, working on a memory verse, or listening to praise music or Bible stories. This means you need to stay off the cell phone! At home, color a picture or make a craft based on the Bible or a godly characteristic. At the dinner table, everyone can share a "high"—a good thing that happened—and a "low"—a bad thing that happened in the day. Use these events as part of your prayers. Tuck your children in each night with a hug, a kiss, and a prayer.

Use everyday living to trigger object lessons for your children. Ask God to open your eyes to situations you can relate to the Bible. For example, when your kids take a bath or give the dog a bath, you can discuss how Jesus washes away our sins. When you're baking, you can talk about what Jesus meant when He called Himself the bread of life. Let them play with a flashlight and think about Jesus, the light of the world.

In a family devotion time you can read a Bible story or devotional, have the children act out a Bible story, and pray together. When children hear you pray, they're learning how to talk to God about everything. If you're struggling with when and how to have a family devotion, let Cindy's story inspire you.

> Mark and I would have loved to send our son, Dominic, to a private Christian school, but our finances would not allow that. So when we sent him to public school, we wondered how were we going to spiritually prepare Dominic for his day ahead.
>
> Mark found his answer easily and announced, "We'll have a morning devotion with him before school each day!" My sweet husband can be *so* optimistic. Although I love him dearly, I thought I could wring his cute little neck for forgetting that his wife had never been a morning person.
>
> I have to admit I was not looking forward to this challenge God had put in front of me, but I hoped for the best. I watched blurry-eyed as Mark enthusiastically shared God's Word with Dominic. He took no more than 15 minutes. They started calling this precious time together "putting on his armor." The

name stuck, and now six-year-old Sophie puts on her armor each morning too.

If someone had told me that I would get up 15 minutes early to lead Dominic in a Bible devotion every day of his school years, I would have laughed. But we are going into his sixth year of school, and we continue to have morning devotions. I thank God for His vision through Mark. And most of all, I thank God for giving me strength and determination to give my son this amazing gift of armor for his daily adventures.

We Teach Our Children to Honor Their Parents

"Honor your father and your mother, that your days may be prolonged in the land which the LORD your God gives you" (Exodus 20:12).

Teaching our two sons to obey us and treat us respectfully is one of our top priorities. It's especially important to Scott, and he will not tolerate even a drop of disrespect. I am so thankful for his leadership and authority in this area!

My kids can see and feel the way I support Scott's leadership when I support his guidelines. This means never saying things such as, "Don't tell Dad, and we'll do it just this one time." It means praising him to my kids when he's away. It means saying, "You know Dad wants you to have chores done today, so that's what we're going to do."

When my husband's gone, he needs me to enforce his guidelines. I know that ultimately if I need to, I can call my husband or make one of my sons call him to report their misbehavior; however, since I'm the one home most with the kids, I'm the one who becomes the enforcer!

Mothers, our children's disobedience will wear us down and destroy our authority in their eyes. And they're really good at wearing us down! "Boys, why do I have to repeat myself? I told you to come inside ten minutes ago...No, you cannot go outside to play. It's time to do your homework. Oh, all right, stop whining; you can go for fifteen minutes... We do not say the word *stupid* in our house. If you say it again, you'll be having a long time-out in your room. Did you hear me? I warned you not to say that word. I mean it; you will have a time-out if you say it again!…"

We have to mean what we say and stand firm. Yes, training our children takes effort and energy, but not training them and not disciplining takes even more energy and will exhaust us in the long run. It will also discredit our authority. Disciplining our children and teaching them to respect us as parents is one of the most loving things we can do for them.

Children need to know how to fit into the larger scope of their family life. When children are little and their needs seem urgent, we can easily put too much focus on them to the detriment of other relationships and responsibilities.

Don't put children before your husband. One husband e-mailed me, saying he wished that when he got home, his wife and children would greet him as enthusiastically as his dog. Instead he feels like an intruder and an interruption in his own home.

We Teach Our Children to Love One Another

Although our sons are four years apart in age, we want them to be one another's best friends. We tell them that in the long run they will always have each other; they will always be brothers. Some days we get glimpses that this will actually happen, such as when they're shooting baskets together or when the older one is reading to the younger one. Other days we wonder if they'll even speak to one another when grown!

Scott has moments of brilliance when disciplining his sons. One day Zachary and Tyler were having a really hard time getting along. So Scott made them hug each other for two minutes while reciting, "Chitwood boys stick together; Chitwood boys stick together." By the end of their forced closeness, they were full of giggles and the fight was forgotten. This might be a good idea for husbands and wives too!

These are just a few of our parenting priorities. Ask God to show you what to prioritize in your family.

When considering what your husband needs on the home front,

this true story has been a good reminder to me that what my husband needs at home might be different from what I need.

As Lacy was racing home with her three little kids after dance lessons, she passed the children's elementary school. Looking toward the school, she saw a car that looked like her husband's car. Looking closer, she saw that it *was* her husband Bill's car. Looking even more closely, she saw that not only was it her husband's car, but sure enough, Bill, was sitting in the driver's seat. *I wonder if he's going to some kind of school meeting he forgot to tell me about. But why would he know about it and not me?* She turned into the parking lot and pulled up next to her husband in his car.

Bill looked surprised to see her and folded the newspaper he'd been reading. He rolled down his window, and she rolled down hers. She asked with curiosity, "Honey, what are you doing here?" Bill looked down, and was quiet a few minutes before responding. "Lacy, I've been stopping here on my way home from work for a few months now. I read the newspaper and just enjoy the peace, quiet, and no talking for about 15 minutes; then I'm ready to go home." They talked for a few minutes and then both directed their cars toward home.

I'm not sure what usually greeted Bill at his home. I'm sure with three children it was lively and busy. But I do know that what Bill was looking for after a long, stressful day was a haven.

This story has stayed with me because it makes me see home from my husband's perspective. It challenges me to be the heart of my home, the one who creates a home that is a place where everyone finds refuge, a place my family can call "home sweet home."

PRAYER GUIDE

Dear Lord,
    Thank You for my role as a homemaker. Help me
to have Your perspective, knowing that the world can
demean and distort this role. Help me to have balance,
knowing I don't have to keep a perfectly clean home,

nor do I get to let things go at home. Give me the strength and energy to be a good steward and manager of the material blessings of our life. Give me wisdom, understanding, and knowledge to establish a home that is a haven for my husband and children. Remind me always that the greatest riches in my home are my family members, and help me love them in a way that shows them You treasure them, and I do too. I pray in Jesus' name. Amen.

9

Accepting Your Man

~⌒~

When I was younger, the life I imagined for myself did not include a pickup truck, but along with my husband, Scott, came numerous trucks! One day Scott and I were riding in his blue pickup truck with no air conditioning and hunting ducks painted on the side. I thought to myself, *Who would have ever thought? This is my life and I couldn't be happier!* Our differences were pronounced, but we found the differences fascinating and exciting. They added spice to our lives!

We entered marriage with so many differences: differences in the way we were raised, different personality types, and male-female differences. Scott was raised in a small town in Minnesota; I was raised in the suburbs of Florida. Scott grew up playing sports; I grew up going to the mall. Scott is an extrovert; I'm an introvert. He likes TV; I like books. He's a night owl; I'm a morning person. Scott likes to go nonstop until he crashes; I like life at an even pace. Not to mention he's a man and I'm a woman!

What differences have you observed between you and your husband? You know from reading this book that Scott and I have "heated discussions," which are often conflicts resulting from our differences. Even couples whose differences aren't as marked as Scott's and mine will inevitably notice the dissimilarities. A husband needs his wife to accept the differences with love.

Leaving Home

God tells us when we get married that we leave behind our families of origin. "For this reason a man shall leave his father and his mother, and be joined to his wife; and they shall become one flesh" (Genesis 2:24). As we consider this verse, remember that God's commands for marriage will always be to protect and foster oneness in marriage.

What is included in the phrase "leave his father and his mother"? First, it means a physical separation. You are now living with your husband, not your parents or a roommate, and you are establishing a new home. Setting up house together means incorporating both of your preferences and being willing to let go of the way you did things previously.

The minute the wedding is over and you're settling into married life, the differences rear their heads. For example, when Scott and I were arranging our first home, Scott wanted a TV in our bedroom. Well, according to my set of rules, TVs did not belong in bedrooms. I explained what seemed so logical to me. If we had a TV in our bedroom, we'd spend less time "sharing" and talking. Not a bad idea to Scott, I'm sure! But he graciously did not express this, and went along with my preference. Several years later, I might add, when a TV entered our bedroom, I welcomed it!

This is just one little example of a difference arising from the ways two people were raised. The differences in customs and habits can be numerous: Your family ate in front of the TV, his family always ate at 6:00 PM at the table. Your family always had roast beef for Christmas dinner; his family had turkey. Your family watched football all day on

Thanksgiving Day; his family played games. Just little things, but the little things can add up. And speaking of holidays, this is a time when the "leaving" part of married life can be hard. This is a time in your married life when you will want to make visits, but it's also a great time to establish your own family traditions.

Second, to leave and be joined together, or as the King James Version reads, "to cleave" to one another, means that your allegiance now belongs to your husband. Your husband needs to know that you choose loyalty to him before you choose loyalty to your mother, your father, your friends, your hobbies, and any other person or activity. In Proverbs 31:11 we find a statement that should be a governing principle in our marriages: "The heart of her husband trusts in her." Cleaving to your husband is one way to assure him that he can readily trust you.

So how do we live this out in marriage? We limit our phone calls and visits to our mothers or best friends. Our husbands can count on us not to malign them to anyone. When our parents are pressuring us to visit them, we tell them we need to check with our husbands first. If we're upset about something, we first turn to our husbands for support and comfort. We defend our husbands if anyone attempts to downgrade them or their ways.

As we move away from our parents, we can continue to obey the commandment to "honor your father and your mother" (Exodus 20:12). We can continue to love them, be involved in their lives, and invite them into ours. In fact, loving your in-laws is one of the greatest gifts you can give your husband.

Leaving and cleaving makes marriage the light to which we're inevitably drawn. Ask God to draw you and your husband together and to hold you together. As you negotiate the differences in your marriage, whether you're considering where to put the TV or where to spend the holidays, pray that the differences will bring delight, not division.

Opposites Attract, Opposites Attack

We've all heard that opposites attract, but very quickly opposites can attack each other. What is initially attractive in our boyfriends can quickly become incredibly annoying in our husbands. We then get caught up in trying to change our husbands or praying for God to change them.

Many men and women marry their opposite. Scott and I definitely fall into that category. Scott is talkative, outgoing, and most alive around people. I too love to have friends over for dinner or enjoy a night out at a restaurant with another couple, but I don't want to be social nearly as often as Scott does. This difference in personalities has inevitably led to some conflicts.

When we owned our first house in Charlotte, I felt as if our house had a revolving door. Scott invited friends over for a cookout every weekend—or so it seemed to me! I, on the other hand, looked forward to having a family night on the weekend, times when just Scott and I and our two sons could spread out blankets on the floor and watch a rented movie. When Scott filled up our weekends with activities, I felt hurt that he didn't want to spend time with just his family. Scott did want to spend time with us, but he also wanted to fill every moment of free time with as much fun as possible. He got frustrated that I didn't want that too!

About halfway through our marriage, Scott and I learned at a class at church about different personality types. What a blessing this was to both of us! Of course we had always realized our personalities were different, but we were stuck in the bad habit of trying to change each other. As we took time to understand that our personalities were part of the way God designed us, we began to accept one another's differences.

Florence Littauer's book *Personality Plus for Couples* provides a profile of four personality types.[1] (The page numbers on the next few pages refer to Florence's book). Although every person has a unique personality created by God, we generally fall into one of these four types. Each person has a predominant personality type, often with one other type being a close second. As you read these descriptions, think about which categories you and your husband fall in to.

The sanguine personality type, also called the Popular Personality, describes those who are the "fun-loving, sunny, outgoing personalities who draw people to them because they seem to be having such a good time... These boisterous individuals bring fun and drama into almost any situation, love the spotlight, and enjoy motivating others. They initiate conversations and can instantly become best friends with everyone in a group... they can also be disorganized, emotional and hypersensitive about what others think of them" (page 19).

The opposite personality type from the sanguine is the melancholy, the Perfect Personality. The melancholy is "deep, thoughtful, introspective, serious, and perfectionistic... These perfectionists thrive on order, and you can depend on them to complete a job on time. But their perfectionism may make them critical or pessimistic, and they drive themselves crazy with their efforts to measure up to their own high standards" (p. 20).

The third personality type is the choleric, the Powerful Personality. These people are "the dynamic leaders of life and their motto echoes Nike's slogan of 'Just do it!'... Their self-discipline and ability to focus make them strong leaders. But their drive and determination can cause them to become workaholics, make them opinionated and stubborn, and leave them insensitive to other's feelings" (page 21).

The opposite of the choleric is the phlegmatic, the Peaceful Personality. Phlegmatics are easygoing, pleasant, and peaceful. Phlegmatics "think in terms of conserving energy and feel that if you ignore something long enough, someone else will do it...Phlegmatics dislike risk, challenge, and surprise and will require time to adapt to changes. Although they avoid situations that are too stressful, they can work well under pressure. However, their lack of discipline and motivation often allow them to procrastinate in the absence of a strong leader" (page 21).

This summary of the four personality types gives you the groundwork for identifying your personality type and your husband's. I'm sure that in numerous situations, whether planning a vacation or organizing daily life with jobs and kids, you can see how these personalities come into play. Remember that whatever personality types are combined in your marriage, God planned it that way, and His will is always good, pleasing, and perfect.

Opposites are naturally attracted to each other. In the case of personality types this means that the sanguine and melancholy often marry, and the choleric and the phlegmatic often become husband and wife. The strengths and weaknesses complement one another to create a balanced couple. The extroverted sanguine is a good match for the more reserved melancholy. Or the decisive choleric complements the easygoing phlegmatic. When we appreciate each other's strengths, we have a marriage filled with peace, strength, and satisfaction.

Of course, instead of complementing one another we can easily misunderstand each other, judge one another for not doing the things the same way, or get frustrated with our spouses for their very different ways of thinking. These responses create strife and disharmony—not at all what God desires for marriage. Ephesians 4:1-3 tells us how to foster unity between a husband and wife: "Therefore I, the prisoner of the Lord, implore you to walk in a manner worthy of the calling with which you have been called, with all humility and gentleness, with patience, showing tolerance for one another in love, being diligent to preserve the unity of the Spirit in the bond of peace."

Let's look at a real-life example. My husband is a sanguine/choleric and I'm a melancholy/phlegmatic—exactly opposite! Scott has a friendly "take charge" personality that is very attractive to me—most of the time! As I've mentioned, Scott is a pilot who's away on business trips most weeks, leaving me in charge on the home front. When Scott returns from his travels, he walks in the door ready to be back in charge. I have a choice about how I will respond to this transition. One choice is to perceive his choleric personality as bossiness and to be easily offended by his strong manner. The other choice is to welcome his powerful presence and be thankful that God has given me a husband who is willing and gifted to lead our family. Believe me, I've made both choices over the years, but understanding how God has uniquely designed each of our personalities has helped me to be thankful for my husband.

Notice that each personality type includes positive and negative traits. For example, sanguines can be disorganized, melancholies can tend to be critical, cholerics can turn bossy, and phlegmatics can procrastinate. It's way too easy for a husband and wife to judge one another and focus on the spouse's weaknesses, especially if their personalities are different. For example, a choleric husband might judge his wife for not taking life more seriously. He might think, *What is wrong with her! There's so much work to be done around this house. We need to get dinner started, the house is a wreck, and the kids haven't done their chores.* Meanwhile, the sanguine wife is in the front yard playing with her kids and visiting with neighbors. She's wondering why on earth her husband doesn't lighten up and come join the fun. When we don't accept each other's differences, we can quickly judge our spouses and at the same time think the way we do things is the right way. This judgment puts a wall between the couple, leading each to feel unaccepted and unloved.

Jesus speaks very clearly about judging:

> Do not judge so that you will not be judged. For in the way you judge, you will be judged; and by your standard of measure, it will be measured to you. Why do you look at the speck that is in your brother's eye, but do not notice the log that is in your own eye? Or how can you say to your brother, "Let me take the speck out of your eye," and behold, the log is in your own eye? You hypocrite, first take the log out of your own eye, and then you will see clearly to take the speck out of your brother's eye (Matthew 7:1-5).

Having a certain personality type does not give either spouse permission to think his or her way is the right way. Nor does it provide either one with the excuse of "that's just the way I am." Each couple must find a balance and rhythm that works for both of them, not just one of them. This story of a choleric husband and a sanguine wife illustrates a couple who was willing to respond in love to the other. The husband's love for his wife made him willing to change his tendency to solve problems and instead to empathize with his wife.

> When Shirley developed a dental disorder known as TMJ, she suffered a great deal of pain and discomfort. One day when the pain was particularly bad, her husband came home and found her in tears. She told him of

her pain and said she was going up to bed because she couldn't stand it any longer.

In his typical Choleric way, Nate immediately began his twenty questions. "What's the matter? When did it start? How did it develop? What are your symptoms? What medications have you taken?" And the questions went on.

Finally, Sanguine Shirley looked at him and said, "Right now I don't care about any of those questions. I need you to sympathize with me, take me up to bed, offer me soda and crackers, put your arm around me, and say, 'I'm sorry you're in pain. Is there anything I can do to help?' "

Amazingly, her husband did just that. Ten minutes later, as he was leaving the room after tucking her in and doing all that she had asked of him, he eagerly asked, "How did I do?"

She responded, "Wonderful, thank you."

And then he acknowledged, "Do you have any idea how hard this was for me not to try and fix your problem?" (pages 152–153).

Once we've identified our personality types, we need to pray about these differences. We ask God to show us how our differences can strengthen our marriages and bless all of us. We can thank God for the specific strengths of our husbands—for the friendly sanguine, organized melancholy, high-energy choleric, or peaceful phlegmatic husband. Let's remember that God designed each of our personalities, knows the strengths and weaknesses of our personalities, and planned our marriages. As we accept each other in love, the differences are blessings, not curses as they sometimes feel.

God Created Man and Woman

Last year we decided to put a pool in our backyard, and it's been such a great addition! My sons swam several times a day, and we had plenty of friends over to share in the fun. The ideal pool scenario for me includes floating around on a raft with my ice-cold Diet Coke. My sons loved having me in the pool with them. However, they would have nothing to do with creating my ideal pool scenario.

Every time I swam with them I had to actually, well...swim. No floating allowed. In fact each time they were in the pool they wanted to play some type of game—sharks and minnows, Marco Polo, and all sorts of competitions they invented. I accommodated at first, but finally I'd had enough. I explained to them that when I was growing up in Florida with a pool in my backyard, my girlfriends and I did not play games every time we got in the pool. We floated, sunbathed, and talked, and the only game we played was pretending we were mermaids. So that's what I as their mother, a former girl, wanted to do in the pool. Needless to say they were quite disappointed in my girlieness.

Even at a young age males and females differ from one another, as my summer pool experience reminded me. You and your husband weren't raised the same way or in the same situation, and in your marriage you'll see countless examples of the differences between a wife and a husband.

It helps to remember that God planned this difference: "Male and female He created them" (Genesis 1:27). If God planned us and fashioned us to be different, we can count on God to have done this for our good and for our advantage. But we don't always feel that way, do we? Many times the differences between my husband and me have made me think, *What is wrong with this man?*

We can take two approaches to the gender differences. First, we can magnify the differences into a negative. Focusing on the differences leads to trying to change or fix our husbands. We've probably all heard that a man goes into a marriage expecting nothing to change. On the other hand, a woman enters marriage expecting to change her man. If we take this negative approach, the differences will divide us rather than complete us.

The second approach, obviously the preferable choice, is to accept the differences. Our husbands long to feel our acceptance of who they are. If we're always trying to change them, they get the message that something is wrong with them. My husband has told me that he sometimes has felt as if I'm never satisfied with him and that I always want him to change. At times like this I ask for his forgiveness and God's.

Accepting the differences means in certain situations we negotiate compromises, while in other situations we lovingly accept our man as is. In fact we can go even one step further by embracing the differences. That's right, not just tolerating the differences, *embracing* them.

Not too long ago I had an opportunity to embrace the differences. Scott was driving with me in the car when I noticed he was going exceptionally fast. I looked at him and looked at the rising speedometer. By the grace of God I didn't say anything about his excessive speed. Scott focused straight ahead and continued to accelerate. *What on earth is he doing? We're just going to the mall, for Pete's sake. It's not a race.* But then I realized how mistaken I was. I looked to my right and saw a truck next to us that was keeping up with our pace. *Ah, it is a race, after all! I should have known.* I just smiled at my husband and kept silent.

Such a little difference, but one that could have been a source of irritation and conflict rather than a chance for a smile. When these situations arise, ask God for patience and a sense of humor.

Men and women differ in many areas, but two seem to create a lot of conflicts in marriages: communication and sex. Let's take a look at how we as wives can approach these two areas.

Communication: The Open Road or a Roadblock?

Communicating is one of the main ways we become intimate with our husbands. Communication can be a road to oneness, but too often couples feel it's a roadblock instead. In fact, "86 percent of those who divorce say that the main problem was deficient communication."[2]

We might look back to our dating days and remember when we had no problem communicating. Courtship was a time of discovering as much as we could about one another. When Scott and I were dating, we worked as high school teachers at the same school. After school we usually spent some time catching up with each other, later that night we'd often have dinner together, and then before going to sleep we'd talk on the phone. That's a lot of talking!

In marriage we can continue the adventure of discovering one another through talking, but we need to accept two things. First, communication in marriage may differ from that in courtship. Second, we need to accept the differences in male/female communication.

From Bride to Wife

When you're dating, the process of getting to know one another becomes one of your top priorities. You spend time together sharing activities and talking. That's what you're all about. Part of you is evaluating and thinking about whether or not you can marry this guy and live happily ever after. Those strong feelings of being in love may carry you through accepting many of the differences in your spouse. At the same time you're trying to show your best side, which is often more accommodating than your usual way of relating.

After being married for some time, you may feel as if the relationship has changed, and you're not sure you like it. You and your husband don't really talk the way you used to. And some of your husband's personality traits or habits are now more irritating than charming. What's happening here?

You're changing from a bride to a wife. There's a difference! Your relationship is becoming more real. Now you see the differences between you and your husband in light of forever. *He's going to want to watch football every Sunday for the rest of his life. That doesn't sound like fun to me. He just sits in front of that TV for hours. What happened to talking?*

Life has changed. You're now married and living life with all its responsibilities. Jobs, homes, and children can take up so much of your energy that you seem to stop growing as a couple. And the most frustrating part may be that it seems perfectly fine with your husband. That's where the acceptance comes into play.

Mature love can accept that marriage is different from dating. Not worse, just different. Mature love can accept that priorities *do* change and that they need to change. A mature wife can accept that the way her husband shows his love now may be through working hard to provide for his family instead of taking you out every week for a long talk over dinner. A wife accepts that after a long week, maybe the activity her husband needs the most is just "zoning" in front of the TV.

Please don't misunderstand me. As I wrote in a previous chapter, marriage is meant to include many forms of love—friendship, romantic, sexual, and unconditional—and the expression of each type includes communication. We as wives need to accept that communication—like anything else in marriage—will be better in some seasons than in others. Sometimes you will enjoy new heights of intimacy, but at other times you and your husband won't have opportunities to talk about much more than the coordination of your busy schedules. Accept the ebb and flow of communication, and find a balance that you and your husband agree on.

Who Knows What They're Thinking?

Tyler was about three years old when he was riding home from preschool with his best buddy, Brooke. Out of the blue, Brooke looked at Tyler and asked, "Tyler, do you love me?" As he looked out the car's window Tyler answered, "Brooke, look at the trees!" Not to be deterred, Brooke asked again, "But Tyler, do you love me?" Tyler firmly answered, "Brooke! Look at the trees!"

Who knows what was going on in the heads of those precious three-year-olds! We might want to say the same thing about our husbands today. Who knows what's going on in their heads—because they don't tell us! One of the most frequent complaints among wives is that their husbands just don't talk to them. Scientists have offered one explanation: Men on average use about half as many words as women per day. That little tidbit of information is helpful, but it's not a very satisfying answer, is it? It doesn't remove our desire to communicate with our husbands. So how do we reach a place where the amount of communication is pleasing to both husband and wife?

We can start by understanding some of the differences in male/female communication. I'm going to make some generalizations about male/female differences, realizing that some people fall into these generalizations, and some don't. But understanding these differences can help us accept one another and communicate more effectively.

Women Share, Men Solve Problems

Conflicts in communication often arise because men and women have different reasons for talking. Women share. Oh, how a husband can dread that word! Will it mean he'll be listening to you ramble for a half hour? Will it mean you'll be telling him all the things he's done wrong? Will it mean you'll add to his to-do list? Will it mean he'll listen and listen and have no idea what the point of the conversation was?

Men are problem solvers. God created them to be fixers. They often assume that what you share with them is a problem you want help solving. The more you talk, the more he feels buried by a dump truck load of problems. He may naturally begin shutting down or getting angry.

'Sometimes my husband feels I'm talking *at* him in a one-sided conversation, especially when my side of the conversation sounds something like this: "Scott, the computer's messing up, and I can't fix it. When you get a chance, could you look at it? Oh, I meant to tell you—the boys have a dentist appointment later today, and it'd be great if you'd take them. If you can't that's okay, just let me know. I just talked to my sister this morning. I really miss her and want to go see her later this month. They said they just got a new digital camera. Maybe we should look into getting one. Then we could send photos to our family."

Scott's response may be the "deer in the headlights" look, or he may simply say, "I cannot process any more." For a long time I just didn't understand that. I thought something was wrong with him. But nothing is wrong—I have to get past the stinkin' thinkin' that expects Scott to think like me. I need to respect the differences in our communication styles.

Understanding that men tend to compartmentalize can really be helpful in marriage. Bill and Pam Farrel offer an amusing and helpful explanation of male/female communication differences in *Men Are Like Waffles—Women Are Like Spaghetti*. A man's thinking is...

> divided up into boxes that have room for one issue and
> one issue only. The first issue of life goes in the first box,
> the second goes in the second box, and so on. The typical

man lives in one box at a time and one box only. When a man is at work, he is at work. When he is in the garage tinkering around, he is in the garage tinkering...As a result, men are problem solvers by nature. They enter a box, size up the "problem," and formulate a solution.[3]

Women, on the other hand, view life, people, and situations as connected. The Farrels explain:

> Women process life more like a plate of pasta. If you look at a plate of spaghetti, you notice that there are lots of individual noodles that all touch one another. If you attempted to follow one noodle around the plate, you would intersect a lot of other noodles, and you might even switch to another noodle seamlessly. That is how women face life. Every thought and issue is connected to every other thought and issue in some way. Life is much more of a process for women than it is for men.[4]

When I remember that Scott tends to organize conversations into boxes, then I understand why he would sometimes say he cannot process any more. He's not trying to avoid conversation with me, as I can mistakenly think. He just wants to take things one step at a time. In the conversation I described above, I've presented four different ideas, which he perceives as problems to solve. I, on the other hand, mostly just want to share! If he can help me, that's great, but usually I don't really want him to do anything. Just stating aloud what's on my plate for the day has given me the outlet I needed, and then I'm ready to face the day. However, Scott feels as I've just shifted all my "problems" onto him.

Communication Solutions

So what do we do with these communication differences? First, be thankful for the differences. Don't assume something is wrong with your husband because he doesn't think the way you do. Wives need to remember that God created the differences. He designed us this way. Scott's ability to focus on one thing at a time enables him to be a great problem solver or fixer. When I think about fixing things, I often think about my computer. I would rather do just about anything other than try to fix a problem with my computer. My husband, on the other hand, can concentrate for hours on fixing the computer. Thank goodness!

Second, respect your husband's need to not talk. That's right. Just leave him alone for a while! This will recharge his batteries, making him more ready to do what you want, which probably includes engaging in a conversation. Give him time and space to work in the yard, zone out in front of the TV, work on the computer, read a book, work on a project, or exercise. Especially during times of stress, your husband needs talk-free time. I've found that if Scott has alone time, he's more likely to want to connect with me.

Third, we can find other outlets for our need to talk. Jesus is our Friend and desires for us to go to Him first with all our thoughts and feelings. He can handle any problem in our lives, and He welcomes us to bring everything to Him. Before you pick up the phone to call a friend, go to God in prayer. Next, we can go to friends to release our talking. Other women understand that just talking is sometimes the best medicine for a frustrating day. They understand that just talking will help us sort out things and feel better.

Fourth, try a different approach to communication with your husband. Communication is certainly important in marriage because it helps develop oneness. I find that if I don't communicate with Scott, I don't feel close to him. However, I've also found that talking to the Lord first is often all I need to do. Ask your husband to let you know when a good time to talk would be. Then wait for your husband to be ready. Let me say that again—*wait!* And as you're waiting, pray!

I can just hear some women saying that if they waited for their husbands, they'd never end up talking. Maybe that's true, but in most cases I don't think that it is. I think most wives get impatient, so they push issues and end up having horrible conversations.

If some time has passed without your husband saying he's ready to talk, bring up your desire to talk in a respectful and loving way. Maybe your husband honestly forgot and did not intentionally try to avoid you. Assume the best of him! Some husbands really would rather avoid talking altogether, but this may stem from their fear of what's going to happen when you talk.

Wives, we can respect our husbands' communication styles by doing one simple thing to help allay their fears: We can tell our husbands what we really need from the conversation. Maybe we just need them to listen for ten minutes. If that's the case, we can tell them up front that they don't have to solve any problems, that just their listening will be helpful to us and makes us feel closer to them. On the other hand, if we need help with a specific problem, we can tell them that. Remember their "boxes"! Present just one situation at a time.

Another idea for communicating comes from a busy wife, mother, and teacher named Michelle:

> Lately, we both have been extremely busy with work, church, and other activities, and we haven't been able to communicate, let alone have any one-on-one time with each other. Eventually, we both begin to feel resentment and frustration with each other. The feelings build and build until one of us realizes that our needs are not being met, and then, you guessed it, a fight ensues.
>
> So on our anniversary date this year, we both discussed ways we can avoid that buildup. I suggested we leave Post-it notes on the bathroom mirror indicating to the other what we need from that person during the week. It could be an overdue hug, some extra patience, or to be greeted at the door by a person instead of by the dog! This way, when life's busyness gets to us, we can make a note to put the other's needs ahead of our own. For me, I literally have to carry that note around or put it in a place where I'll be reminded to do it. So far, so good!

Maybe this idea would work for your marriage. Another couple I heard of keeps journals that they exchange at the end of the week. Maybe you can come up with other ideas together. Find what works for both of you.

A Time to Be Silent, a Time to Speak

Wives, let's be careful about how much we talk. We women tend to turn to talking as a solution. When we're stressed, we talk. When we don't understand something, we talk. When we want to feel loved, we talk.

I want you to think about your talking. Might God possibly want you to exercise self-control in your conversations? Part of the fruit of the Spirit is self-discipline. Just because we're generally designed to be talkers, women do not have license to speak whatever and whenever we want. God has a wealth of comments on talking in the Bible: "When there are many words, transgression is unavoidable, but he who restrains his lips is wise" (Proverbs 10:19). This is just one of many references to talking in the book of Proverbs.

We live in a culture that allows us to say almost anything we think or feel, but as always, we as Christians must go to God's Word for guidance. Ecclesiastes refers to "a time to be silent and a time to speak" (Ecclesiastes 3:7). If we are going to speak to our husbands about a difficult situation, we need to proceed carefully and prayerfully. If we go to God, honestly submitted to His will, God will lead us in the paths He wants us to take.

Laughter, the Best Medicine

"A joyful heart is good medicine" (Proverbs 17:22). Sometimes the best way to embrace the male/female differences is just to laugh. The longer I've been married, the easier I've been able to laugh at situations that would have angered me previously. I know that sometimes I can get so wrapped up in a frustrating situation that I just want to be mad. Can you relate to that? That's when I need to turn to God, confess my sin, and ask Him to take control of my thoughts. "For as he thinks within himself, so he is" (Proverbs 23:7). The Holy Spirit really can transform a tense situation into one that brings laughter. One day Scott and I were talking on the phone after he'd been away for several days. I was feeling worn out, but he was not very sympathetic. I told him he just did not understand or appreciate all I had to do while he was away. I ended angrily with, "You just do not get the big picture!"

Scott's teasing response was, "Melanie, do you think *you* are the big picture?" I was silent for a minute, and then I just started to laugh. How right he was! I was getting way too wrapped up in myself, and Scott's answer gave me a new perspective. He helped me realize I was blowing things out of proportion and that everything would be fine.

As we accept the differences in a husband's and wife's communication styles, we can work to communicate in a way that both husband and wife find agreeable. Communication can be an open road to greater intimacy.

Sexual Intimacy

The differences between men and women become even more obvious in the way we think about sex. And that's the point. Men think about sex—a lot!

One day I was telling my husband about the errands I needed to do. One of those errands was taking my van to have the tires rotated.

My husband said to me, "I'd like to rotate your tires."

"No thanks, honey. I know you know how to do that and I know you could do it, but I also know how you have a lot of other things to do too. I'll just go get it done. It won't take too long."

Then he said it again. "I'd like to rotate your tires." Only this time I noticed the suggestive tone in his voice. The way he was grabbing me was also a hint.

I'm talking about tires and he's talking about sex! How did this happen! I wondered with pure amazement.

Scenarios like this can easily lead wives to think that all husbands think about is sex. And that kind of thinking can lead wives to be critical of their husbands for wanting sex all the time. The truth is that most men *do* think about sex frequently, and that's the way God designed them. Sex is very important to a man, and it's very important in a marriage. This is the one gift God has given to a married couple to be enjoyed exclusively by the two of them. Just them. In fact, it's so important to a marriage that God says we should not withhold sex from one another.

In an earlier chapter we saw that in Genesis God said that through physical intimacy a husband and wife become one. "For this reason a man shall leave his father and his mother, and be joined to his wife; and they shall become one flesh. And the man and his wife were both naked and were not ashamed" (Genesis 2:24-25). This oneness refers not just to physical intimacy, but to all other forms of intimacy as well. With this in mind, doesn't it make sense that a man would want to have sex with his wife?

If we think about it, we know that yes, it does. Often the problem for women stems from the differences we discussed in the previous section. Men compartmentalize while women connect everything. Men can hop into their sex "box" in the blink of an eye. Women, however, have a much harder time making the transition—for example, from mother to lover. Also, women tend to want an emotional connection to precede the physical connection.

> Just as many men fail to understand how important it is to become deeply involved in all emotional aspects of his wife's world, many women fail to understand how deeply sex can be connected to emotional oneness for their husbands. Part of this is due to the fact that many men do a very poor job articulating the incredibly intense and immense sensations that are occurring within them far beyond what is happening on the physiological level. To many men, being one sexually is *the* place where they feel most one—most naked and unashamed—with their mates.[5]

My husband and I often get stuck in the what-comes-first rut. I don't want to make love until I feel emotionally connected to my husband. He feels emotionally connected when we make love. Can you relate to this dynamic? I need to remember that sex is not just a physical act. It's a way for me to say to my husband, "I accept you, I'm here for you, and I want to be close to you." Most importantly, it's a way for me to love my husband the way he needs to be loved.

Talking about sex can be very helpful. We can tell our husbands what helps us set our minds on sex, and we need to be willing to listen to our husbands express their needs about sex too. Many women, myself included, are willing to work on different areas of our marriages, but frankly, we don't want to spend a whole lot of time working on differences in the area of physical intimacy.

Anne and Mark were willing to listen to and respond to one another's needs. Anne told her husband...

> that he was a great husband, but that this one thing made her feel very uncared for. She told him that his willingness to tell her a realistic time when he'd be home and stick to it was—for her—one of the most important signals of his love. Mark understood and that became a top priority for him.
>
> Now, years later, Mark sat down with Anne and told her that he was concerned about the drop-off in their sex life. He drew a parallel to Anne's need for him to be home when he promises. He said, "I could be a great husband but not do this one thing that is really important to you, and I'd still fail at making you feel loved. Having sex like we used to, having you be responsive to me, is the same thing for me."[6]

Are you listening to what your husband is telling you about his desire to be physically intimate with you? Is this the one way your husband will feel most loved? Does he know that you desire him and only him?

In our world, sex is rarely what God intended it to be. Sex is not ever "just sex," as Satan would have us believe. So we have to think purposefully about what God *did* intend it to be. Obviously it's for procreation, but God could have created other ways to continue the human race. But He didn't. He gave us the gift of sex to enjoy with one another, to express all that we are to one other person, to offer our vulnerability to one another, and to demonstrate our love. Sex as God intended it is a way for a husband and wife to say again and again, I choose you. Sex "seals the deal" of marriage.[7]

It Was Very Good

When we think about our differences, we need to remember that this was God's plan. "Male and female He created them" (Genesis

1:27). And God called it good: "God saw all that He had made, and behold, it was very good" (Genesis 1:31). Whatever your differences, including the way you were raised, personality differences, or gender differences, accepting these differences with grace brings unity, not division, to your marriage.

PRAYER GUIDE

Lord, I pray that I will always be drawn to my husband and that my allegiance will be to him first, before any other human relationships. If I need to leave behind anything in my life in order to cleave more tightly to my husband, reveal that to me. Help us to assume the best of each other. Help us to embrace our many differences in lifestyle, personalities, and gender. Especially in communication and sexual intimacy, I pray that You will bind Satan from our marriage. I know that You intend for these two areas to bring unity, not division. Help us to respect each other in love as we develop oneness in our marriage. Lord, we love You and trust that these differences were designed for our good. I especially pray that in a world filled with so much sexual immorality, we will guard our hearts, and our desire will always be for one another. I ask these things in Your name. Amen.

10

Surviving the Storms

September 11, 2001. A day we now know as 9/11. A day that began like any other day for people across the nation.

I remember getting my carpets cleaned and then going to Ginny's house. Such an ordinary day. Before I left the house, Scott had turned on the news, but I didn't pay much attention. About an hour later Scott called me at Ginny's and with a firm and somber voice said, "You need to turn on the news. Now." So we did. Like every other American, we could not believe what we saw. Planes crashing, the Twin Towers tumbling down, speculations of terrorists, distraught screams, panic, mayhem.

I hurried home, where we kept the TV on all day. The phone rang off the hook as family and friends called seeking reassurance that Scott was home, not flying an airplane for US Airways that day as he so often would be. With heavy hearts we thanked God that Scott was home, but at the same time we grieved for the incredible losses we witnessed. I called my brother, who lives in New York City, and just quietly cried as I heard his voice and assurances that he was safe.

Scott knew immediately that this day would change the airline industry. He told me this would probably mean the end of his job with US Airways. We were consumed with the tragedy, so we really didn't dwell on his job. However, we knew that in the days and weeks that followed, many pilots would lose their jobs. Sure enough, on December 2, 2001, Scott was "furloughed" or laid off from US Airways.

We knew that in light of the losses experienced by so many on 9/11, our loss was minor, but it was still a heavy loss for us. Scott lost more than a job. He lost a dream. For ten years Scott had pursued the dream of being a commercial airline pilot. He had worked diligently, and we both had made sacrifices. What was to become of those dreams?

This was the most challenging storm we had faced so far in our marriage. Every marriage will weather the dark and tumultuous days of storms. If you haven't yet, you will. That's just part of life. The storms come in many forms: sicknesses, financial hardships, aging of parents, wayward children, damaging addictions, and infidelity. During storms you'll discover the strength of your marriage. You'll discover whether your marriage is built on the sand or on the Rock. The storms will either tear you apart or strengthen you.

Remember the vows you said on your wedding day? "I, Melanie, take you, Scott, to be my husband; to have and to hold, from this day forward; for better, for worse; for richer, for poorer; in sickness and in health; to love and to cherish till death do us part, and hereto I pledge you my faithfulness." When I said those vows, my heart was bursting with love, hope, and happiness. I sure wasn't thinking about any hard roads ahead, and I'm sure you weren't on your wedding day either. Although we can't imagine what "for worse" will mean on the day we say our vows, we can be sure that God already knew on that wedding day, and He knows right now what's in our future. He is with us during the storms.

What storms have you and your husband weathered? What were your responses during the crises? If you haven't weathered a storm yet, let the lessons of this chapter strengthen the bond you and your husband share and prepare you for any storms ahead.

Who Do You Say That I Am?

The story of Jesus calming the storm shows what Jesus can do in the storms of our lives.

> Leaving the crowd, [the disciples] took Him along with them in the boat, just as He was; and other boats were with Him. And there arose a fierce gale of wind, and the waves were breaking over the boat so much that the boat was already filling up. Jesus Himself was in the stern, asleep on the cushion; and they woke Him and said to Him, "Teacher, do You not care that we are perishing?" And He got up and rebuked the wind and said to the sea, "Hush, be still." And the wind died down and it became perfectly calm. And He said to them, "Why are you afraid? Do you still have no faith?" (Mark 4:36-40).

The storms of life help make you serious about your relationship with Christ. You have a choice. You can choose bitterness, or you can choose faith. Bitterness plants seeds of doubt, anger, blame, and betrayal. Your thoughts become filled with stinkin' thinkin'. *What happened to "happily ever after"? What did we do to deserve this? Why did You allow this, God? Why didn't my husband take steps to prevent this situation?*

When Scott lost his job, I knew that the only way that our family would survive the challenge was to choose faith, to choose to depend completely on the power, comfort, and assurance of Jesus. Faith sees the storms but clings to Jesus. Jesus asked Peter a question that we all have to answer in the storms: "But who do you say that I am?" (Mark 8:29). I had to answer that question every day when Scott was unemployed. I told God, *You are Lord of lords and King of kings, and nothing is too difficult for You.* And God answered, *Then trust Me in this and see what I can do.*

Looking for God

I began to look for evidence of God's provision during this time. The first provision was the peace I had. I just knew that we were going to be okay. I can't explain the peace other than to say it was supernatural, for I had many questions: How can we afford our living expenses? Will Scott be able to find another flying job? Will I have to go back to work? Will we have to sell our house? Will we have to move?

I've heard a saying that Jesus will either calm the sea or He will calm me. I found this to be so true. Jesus gave me His calm down deep in my heart as God gave me a deep sense of peace when Scott went through what turned out to be six months of unemployment. That doesn't mean that I didn't have times when I had to fight for that peace. Sometimes I felt depleted, sometimes I had to wrestle my thoughts of fear and take those thoughts captive to God, and sometimes I would just pour out my heart and my tears to God.

I love the faithful and courageous words of Moses to the Israelites as they faced the Egyptian army. They thought they were trapped by the Red Sea, but Moses told them to watch what God could do! "But Moses said to the people, 'Do not fear! Stand by and see the salvation of the LORD which He will accomplish for you today; for the Egyptians whom you have seen today, you will never see them again forever. The LORD will fight for you while you keep silent'" (Exodus 14:13-14).

During our challenge, I tried every day to be in a place where I could say, *I'm not sure where this will end up, but I am sure of You, Lord. I can't wait to see what You will do!*

Let God Be Your Life Preserver

My husband was wrestling with fears, disappointment, and questions. He felt a huge responsibility to provide for our family. He was dealing with the incredible disappointment of losing his job and what might mean the death of his dream. He did not need me unloading all my fears on him. He was doing his best to stay above water, so I knew he could not be my life preserver. I had to let God fill that role. I had to cling to His promises. "Jesus said to them, 'With people this is impossible, but with God all things are possible'" (Matthew 19:26).

As I looked for God's provision during this difficult time, I learned to depend on God in a way that I didn't when times were easier and less stressful. So the second provision during this time was seeing that God truly was all I needed. I witnessed firsthand that even when the world seems to be spinning out of control, God is sovereign and in control.

Friends to Lift You Up

A third way God provided was through friendship. Scott and I are part of an awesome church, and we felt our church family reaching out with arms of love, support, and prayer. They truly bore our burdens, as Galatians 6:2 teaches.

Then in an unusual turn of events that was orchestrated by God, our best friends came to live with us for a while. Adam was a furloughed pilot with Continental. He and his family had left Charlotte for him to work in Guam for a few years. Knowing they'd eventually return to Charlotte, they kept their home and rented it out for a year. When Adam was furloughed, they returned to Charlotte. They didn't want to displace the renters from their home, so having them stay with us was the natural thing to do.

Chere and I are the best of friends, their twin boys, Cade and Carter are the same age as Zachary, and their youngest, Callie, is the same age as Tyler. Our families love being together, so during this stressful time God gave us the gift of being with our best friends! Adam and Scott both were looking for new piloting jobs, so they drew support and knowledge from each other. Chere and I had each other to talk to, vent to, and pray with. The kids had best buddies to play with every day!

The greatest gift that God knew we needed was one we'd always enjoyed with the Wassers—laughter! Even during this stressful time, we joked and laughed our way through.

Love Your Husband by Believing in Him

As I prayed during this time, I saw that God could use it to make our marriage stronger. I knew that the stress could drive us apart or pull us together. I really tried to love Scott the way he needed to be loved. I saw that he really needed an encourager. More than ever before, I tried to communicate to him in many ways that I believed in him. As a result, the fourth provision during this time was a stronger love binding us together in our marriage.

One of the primary ways you can be what your husband needs during a crisis is to believe in him. A man is driven to know "he has what it takes."[1] You have many ways to communicate that you believe in your husband, and one of the best ways to let him know you believe in him is to be physically intimate. Most men would agree that during a stressful time, sex is a great way to relieve the pressure they feel. When a man knows his wife desires him physically, he feels affirmed for who he is, and he's assured that regardless of what happens, his wife believes in him.

> Home is the most important place for a man to be affirmed. If a man knows that his wife believes in him, he is empowered to do better in every area of his life. A man tends to think of life as a competition and a battle, and he can energetically go duke it out if he can come home to someone who supports him unconditionally, who will wipe his brow and tell him he can do it. As one of our close friends told me, "It's all about whether my wife thinks I can do it. A husband can slay dragons, climb mountains, and win great victories if *he* believes his *wife* believes that he can."[2]

During stressful times, as you draw strength from God, you can stand firmly beside your husband, lending him your strength. "Two are better than one because they have a good return for their labor. For if either of them falls, the one will lift up his companion. But woe to the one who falls when there is not another to lift him up" (Ecclesiastes 4:9-10).

A Change in Perspective

Scott's unemployment came in the shadow of the tragedy of 9/11. Although we knew no one involved personally, we grieved with so many who had suffered losses that day. Scott's job as a pilot made the "what if" factor hit close to home. What if Scott had been one of the pilots of the hijacked planes?

A fifth provision from God in a crisis is an eternal perspective. You can pray to see your situation through the eyes of your loving Father. Although you see pain and confusion, you know that God causes all things to work together for good. Even when you don't understand why something happens, you know that you can trust your heavenly Father.

A crisis can give you a perspective that revives your thankfulness for what you do have. You ask yourself what matters most in your marriage. For us the answers were that we love each other and communicate that every day, that we don't take the strength of our marriage for granted, that we gather our children into a loving circle of our family, that we can get through whatever life brings us as long as we are united with each other in God's love.

Sure, Scott had lost a job, but the most valuable parts of our life were intact. At a time when not everyone could say that, we were thankful to the very core of our beings for the way God provided for us.

Sometimes a husband needs you as his wife to be the one to help keep things in perspective. This was one way I supported Scott during this time. I prayed constantly for him to keep his eyes on God, to be reassured of God's love and promises for him, and to have an eternal perspective.

New Priorities

The new perspective we both gained during this crisis led to new questions. At the time we were committed Christians, but we were equally committed to a nice, comfortable life. I do not think material things are bad at all. I just think for us they needed to have their right place. This crisis was an opportunity for us to examine our priorities.

Scott asked questions of God: *What are You trying to teach me? What direction do You want my life to take? Do You want me to stay in flying? Do You want me to pursue another career path? Is my life bringing You glory, Lord?* And in seeking answers, Scott changed. He became a man who is wholeheartedly devoted to God, a man after

God's own heart. God had been a part of his life for many years, but now God became his top priority. This trial was a time when Scott set his eyes on the supreme goals in life: knowing God, enjoying Him, and glorifying Him.

We could have missed the opportunity, but Scott took it, and our marriage has been better because of it. I believe Satan was fighting to keep us grasping for false and empty dreams, but Satan did not defeat us. We stood firm, and God fought for us.

Whirlwinds from Within

Maybe you think you could survive a storm that comes from an outside force, such as a job loss, financial troubles, trouble with a child, or life-threatening illness. But what about a crisis in your marriage that your husband caused? What if his alcoholism, workaholism, pornography addiction, or infidelity is the cause of the storm? Could you survive this storm?

A crisis that your husband causes will shake the love, trust, and security you have known in your marriage. You may be overwhelmed with rage and pain. You may think you could never want to stay in your marriage.

I want to share with you a story about two Christians whose marriage was rocked by infidelity. I'm so thankful for their willingness to share this story, and I hope that their honesty will help any marriage threatened by the same storm. This is a true story, but I've changed their names to protect their privacy. I begin to tell their story by including Tina's actual journal entries.

September 3—I think our marriage is in a better place. We are trusting God more than we ever have before. We've already had so many struggles in our marriage, but in the last two years we both feel it's gotten stronger than ever. I think it's because our faith has grown so much.

September 25—I'm learning I can't stray very much from God's Word. I just don't have peace if I do. I begin to believe too many lies about my husband and children. Satan is feeding me many lies. I begin to get resentful of not having time to myself. I get too obsessed with material things. I get filled with the ideas of the world. When I have an eternal perspective and fill my mind with God's Word, I am reminded of what matters most—God, my husband, and my children.

October 16—Steve told me this morning that he broke our marriage vows. Oh, I hate him right now. I want to hurt him the way he's hurt me. I want to verbally tear him apart and go and be with someone else to show him what it feels like.

I have to do this through Your grace and forgiveness that only You can give me. You're the only One who can help me to forgive. I need to cling to You for everything, Lord. I have to look at him as one of the "least of them," like You say in Matthew.

October 16 (later that night)—He is just a man. A sinner. I won't let him ruin what I have in You, Lord. I'm Your child, and You love me. I will not doubt in You because of what he did to me. I will not turn my back on You and all that You are to me. Faith is believing in the unseen. I know You love me. I know You love my kids.

You can work good out of evil. People meant it for evil, but You, Lord, can make it good. I must rest in Your peace, grace, and understanding. Help me not to be vengeful, hurtful, and spiteful. Help me to know what to say to the kids when they see us fighting. Give me my portion today.

Thank You for the friendship I have with Kim. That I confided in her, that she loves me and Steve, and mostly that she loves You and encourages us to do Your will.

I looked up this verse about loving the least of these for You, God. That's what I have to do with Steve.

> "For I was hungry, and you gave Me something to
> eat; I was thirsty, and you gave Me something to drink;
> I was a stranger, and you invited Me in; naked and you
> clothed Me; I was sick, and you visited Me; I was in prison
> and you came to Me."

Then the righteous will answer Him, "Lord, when did we see You hungry, and feed You, or thirsty, and give You something to drink? And when did we see You a stranger, and invite You in, or naked, and clothed You? When did we see You sick, or in prison, and come to You?"

The King will answer and say to them, "Truly I say to you, to the extent that you did it to one of these brothers of Mine, even the least of them, you did it to Me" (Matthew 25:35-40).

October 17—You gave me Your supernatural love for Steve this morning. I was able to put my arms around him and ask why and how he could do this to me. It was very freeing. I wanted to think of him as scum of the earth because he sinned against me, but I was convicted that You don't treat me that way, Lord, even though You know all my sin against You.

It hurts that Steve did such an intimate act with someone else. An act that is meant only for us. That hurts. I feel rejected, hurt, and taken advantage of. Please don't let me wallow in self-pity. It hurts my pride too. I want to learn and grow from this.

I told Steve that I have kept him at a distance for a long time, really for most of our marriage. I wasn't sure if it was because I wasn't sure if I really loved him or if it was just safer that way.

But in the last two years I've had a heart change, and then this happens. O Lord, make it for good. Take my misery and work it out for Your glory because I believe in You and Your healing power. I choose to focus on You. I cast all my burdens on You. They're Yours now.

October 18—Lord, I continue to have divine appointments with You, and they're exactly what I need. Yesterday we turned on the Christian radio station, and right that moment on the broadcast was a sermon on forgiveness. The pastor used an example that I know was meant for us to hear. He told about a husband who had an affair and hid it from his wife for a long time. Finally, he couldn't bear the guilt anymore, so he told his wife. She wept and wept, but later she told him she loved him, she had promised herself to him, and she would keep that promise. She forgave him. Lord, You are truly amazing. I know You wanted me to hear that.

October 20—We met with a Christian counselor today. I think he's the one we're supposed to be with. He said we can save our marriage and make it better than ever. I believe him. He offered me some initial advice about rebuilding our marriage.

1. Know where my husband is at all times and be able to talk to him on the phone when he is gone.

2. Be interested in his job and what's going on there because that's where he spends most of his time.

3. Make him my priority, second only to God.

4. Plan a date night every week and do different things.

5. Be spontaneous.

6. Pray and kiss in front of the kids.

7. Help my husband find his passion.

October 23—I trust You, Lord. Steve and I kissed this morning on the couch the way we kissed ten years ago. I had a tingling in my stomach. It was magical and wonderful and from You.

Tina wrote these journal entries two years ago. When Tina and I talked recently about what she and Steve experienced, these are the insights she shared:

> I knew then that the world would see what I was going through as something evil and awful. And it was absolutely heartbreaking. But I prayed to see it through God's eyes. I believe that God can make all things new, that God can work all things to our good if we believe in Him.
>
> God transformed our marriage as I rested in Him and trusted His plan for my life. It was not my effort or Steve's that changed things. The problem in the past was that both of us were trying

too hard in our own strength to fix things or make them right. But the whole time God was saying, *Okay, let Me change things, let Me have control instead of you trying to control everything.* I believe the hard work was abiding in *Him* and trusting *Him* to meet all of my needs, not Steve and not myself.

Our biggest challenge as Christians is to remember who we are in Christ and see how He sees us. We must renew our minds daily so that our minds will be transformed. That is truly what we need to live the victorious life that God promises.

And God worked all things together for good because we believed in Him rather than in ourselves. My life with Steve and my children is stronger and better. And the issues I kept dealing with are gone. I can honestly say that I would go through it all again rather than live the mediocre life I was living before.

Tina and Steve are truly a thriving couple now and would be the first to tell you that their marriage is better than ever. Their example offers several lessons for us.

Cry Out to God

Tina recorded her cries to God in her journal. She was completely honest and vulnerable with God about her thoughts and feelings. She also asked God for what she needed. God heard her cries and provided her with love, forgiveness, and joy. She truly has a new song to sing about her marriage.

> I waited patiently for the LORD; and He inclined to me and heard my cry. He brought me up out of the pit of destruction, out of the miry clay, and He set my feet upon a rock making my footsteps firm. He put a new song in my mouth, a song of praise to our God; many will see and fear and will trust in the LORD (Psalm 40:1-3).

Seek God with All Your Heart

When I read Tina's journal entries, I'm amazed by her wholehearted desire to obey God. Many women in her place would have immediately turned to the world's way of dealing with an affair by leaving the marriage. After all, she had grounds for leaving her husband. Instead, she sought God with a heart that was willing to obey regardless of what happened. Jeremiah 29:13 tells us how to seek God: "You will seek Me and find Me when you search for Me with all your heart."

Focus on Your Own Obedience

Tina stayed in the marriage because she knew that was what God wanted her to do. The only guarantee she had was that God would be with her and would bless her obedience. The blessing might be a restored marriage, but it might not be. She focused on abiding in Christ, resting in His love and strength. She committed to forgiving Steve and loving him with God's love. She did not know then that God would bless her with a restored marriage and a changed husband.

Communicate with Your Spouse

Another lesson from Tina and Steve is to communicate, communicate, communicate. You might be tempted to run away from the one who hurt you, but you will need to do just the opposite of what your feelings tell you.

Just a few days after Steve told Tina about his affair, they went on a previously planned family vacation. Tina said that every inch of her did not want to go, but again she prayed and asked God for guidance. She went, and because she did they had hours to talk, cry, and pray together.

Seek Godly Counsel

One of the first things Tina did after Steve confessed his affair to her was to go to friends for comfort, support, and advice. These were friends who knew both her and her husband, and they loved God. She knew that she could count on these friends to offer godly advice based on God's Word. She also could trust that they would keep their situation confidential while they prayed for Tina and Steve's marriage.

They also found a Christian counselor. They met with this counselor for almost a year as they worked through the devastation caused by Steve's affair. They both said they cannot emphasize enough how important it was to have a *Christian* counselor. Their counselor gave them practical advice based on God's truth as they pressed forward in their marriage.

The Lord Is Good

We've looked at two kinds of storms, one external and the other internal. Both types could easily destroy a marriage. However, I hope the stories in this chapter have encouraged you and given you hope in the trials of your own marriage. Your circumstances are different from Tina's or mine, but God knows them. In fact, He knew about your particular storm long before it ever happened.

One time during Scott's early piloting days, he rented a Cessna and flew me to Memphis to visit my sister. I was excited to fly in such a small plane and to have my very own husband as the pilot! While we were there, the weather took a turn for the worse, and a winter storm was unexpectedly on its way. Scott was a novice pilot, and I could tell that the prospects of ice or snow were making him pretty scared. He called his flight instructor several times for advice—which made me quite nervous! That night neither of us slept well as we worried about flight conditions the next day. We woke up at 4:00 AM to go the airport. As Scott readied the plane, I noticed how worried he seemed, so I tried not to aggravate him with unnecessary questions, such as whether he thought we were going to crash and die. I remember thinking that if something did happen, then I'd be where I wanted to be—right next to my husband.

That's the way I've felt during the storms in our marriage. The only place I want to be is right next to my husband. I've witnessed time and time again that God can use the storms in our marriage to draw Scott and me closer together. Sometimes a storm is the most effective means to accomplish the most rewarding closeness.

God uses the trials in another way too. Through them He draws us closer to Him, both individually and as a couple. If we cling to the Lord during hard times, we will come out on the other side with a new perspective of what marriage is all about. We usually enter into marriage with some of our own ideas about living happily ever after, but the happiness we seek tastes much sweeter on the other side of some hardship.

Imagine you've been dieting for two weeks, eating only salad and vegetables and lean protein, as the popular diets these days promote. Then you finally allow yourself a little treat, which for me would be a chocolate chip cookie! Can you imagine how yummy that cookie would taste? It would taste so incredibly delicious that you would say it was the best cookie you'd ever had.

We may think the best of times are the happiest times, but the Lord turns that idea upside down, as He so often does. Times of brokenness in our marriage can be the very experiences that shape us and cause us to enjoy the sweetest fellowship with the Lord and with each other that we'll ever know. That's when we'll be able to say with complete faithfulness, "O taste and see that the LORD is good!" (Psalm 34:8).

PRAYER GUIDE

Dear Lord,

We know that we will face storms in our marriage. Lord, I pray that the storms will draw us together, not divide us. I pray that through any hardships, challenges, or stress that we face individually or as a couple, we will come out on the other side closer to one another and closer to You. Help us not to be anxious or fearful during a storm. Instead, let us stand firmly on our Rock, with You, Lord, as our firm foundation. Let us have peace that passes human understanding as we draw on Your supernatural strength. We know that You can bring good out of horrible situations.

I especially pray that You will protect both of us from sexual temptation. Help us both to keep our marriage bed undefiled in thought, word, and action.

May we have desire only for one another, and may our sexual intimacy satisfy both of us.

Give us the grace to forgive one another when we transgress against one another. We know that because You have forgiven us, we can forgive each other in Jesus' name. Amen.

11

Better Than Ever, Better Together

～⌒◦⌒～

Earlier in this book we looked at Adam and Eve in Genesis. We saw that they succumbed to temptation, causing their relationship and all marriages that have followed to fall short of God's perfect plan.

But God in His love never leaves us alone. He sent His Son, Jesus, as Immanuel, God with us. Now as we abide in Christ we have God's Spirit empowering us to be obedient in our marriages and enabling us to live in God's truth. Only by His strength are we able to live out the principles in this book.

Satan continues to attack marriages and, in too many cases, has done a good job of keeping couples from God's perfect plan. Earlier in this book we learned that "the thief comes only to steal and kill and destroy" (John 10:10), and Satan has stolen God's joy and purpose from many Christian marriages.

Many couples spend so much time and energy attacking each other that they are diverted from some of God's main purposes of marriage. First, marriage is meant to foster individual spiritual growth. Second, marriage is to be an example of God's covenant love. Third, a married couple is to live the adventure of serving God together.

First Things First

When God began to transform me and my marriage, I was serving in several ministries in my church. These were good things; however, I began to see at the time that they were really taking away from the ministry God had for me at home.

God asked me to look closely at my motives for serving outside my home. I clearly saw that while I did love God, and that was certainly one motive of serving, it was not my primary motive. I was mainly motivated by a desire to find significance, praise, and acceptance, needs that were not being met at home. My home life was not rewarding because of strife between Scott and me and because we weren't very thankful for each other. Naturally, I found serving other people much more rewarding.

God began opening my eyes to the ministry He called me to first, which was serving my husband and children before serving others. I'm not at all advocating being selfishly isolated from the body of Christ. I just know that I had to put first things first. God promised that my reward would be found in the contentment of obeying Him. He showed me that so much of the constant tension between Scott and me resulted from my unwillingness to obey Him by following the principles of a godly wife. As I began to set my eyes on Jesus and practice new behavior in my marriage, one of the rewards was a marriage filled with greater peace, joy, and intimacy.

Women can easily become victims of one of Satan's lies that says we'll find greater significance outside our own front doors. As I set my eyes on Christ, I have an eternal perspective, one that knows that a ministry to my family is God's will for me as a wife. Being right in the center of God's will, not ahead of it and not behind it, is the most satisfying and fulfilling place to be.

Refining Our Character

Marriage can actually be a training ground where our character is refined, and we become more like Christ. In Malachi 3:2 we're told that God is "like a refiner's fire." God uses the fire, or challenges in marriage, to refine our character. The *Life Application Study Bible* explains this refining process.

> In the process of refining metals, the raw metal is heated with fire until it melts. The impurities separate from it and rise to the surface. They are skimmed off, leaving the pure metal. Without this heating and melting, there could be no purifying. As the impurities are skimmed off the top, the reflection of the worker appears in the smooth, pure surface. As we are purified by God, his reflection in our lives will become more and more clear to those around us.

Marriage is fertile soil for spiritual growth as day in and day out we come face-to-face with many opportunities to choose our own selfish ways or God's ways.

The very ordinary course of a wife's day brings opportunities to refine her character. Just today I am struggling with my attitude as my husband's work schedule has changed—again. He was supposed to be home Wednesday night, but now it's Friday and because of a malfunctioning plane I'm still not sure when he'll be home.

So how will I handle this small challenge? Will I be gracious and loving with my husband, knowing he's frustrated too? Will I feel sorry for myself as I get my sons to yet another basketball practice and baseball game? Will I be resentful as I walk the two dogs, something he would normally do?

I know these small obstacles may sound petty, but I want to be honest about what's in my heart this morning. This is the opportunity God has given me this morning to refine me. I have tears in my eyes because really I just want my husband home! I don't want to be refined! And then God brought me this verse this morning: "You shall remember all the way which the LORD your God has led you in the wilderness these forty years, that He might humble you, testing you, to know what was in your heart, whether you would keep His commandments or not" (Deuteronomy 8:2). After reading this verse, I prayed that God would till the soil in my heart so He would find a heart fully yielded and committed to Him. God gave me His strength to respond in a way that glorified Him.

What challenges has marriage brought to you? What opportunities has God presented to help you grow in spiritual maturity? In everyday situations and in crises we make choices to walk in the flesh or walk in the Spirit. Choosing to walk in the Spirit leads to growth and maturity. We can choose complaining or thankfulness, forgiveness or resentment, patience or irritability, love or selfishness. Hebrews 6:1 commands us to "press on to maturity." Each choice we make in the Spirit—in obedience to the Holy Spirit and in the strength of the Holy Spirit—leads us to maturity.

Mandy Ferguson remembers a time when her brokenness helped her to press on to maturity.

> I woke up Sunday morning with a really severe headache. But getting back in bed was not an option as I had several commitments I could not back out of. I had to help at the church's baptism that morning, and I had told friends that I would bring a meal to them. All I could think was that if my husband, Butch, would just help me, I could get these things done.
>
> Although Butch was willing to help, he had made commitments for the day too. So as the day progressed, my pounding headache reminded me that Butch was not helping me the way I needed him to. And each time I thought this my anger and resentment grew. By the end of the day we had yelled at each other countless times, and we went to bed hardly speaking.
>
> I could not fall asleep, so I finally just got out of bed and went out into the living room where I tried to pray. Mostly I cried. I lay down on the foyer and looked up at the windows where I could see the light. I poured out my heart to God, telling Him that I was tired of feeling

this way about Butch, tired of being mad at him for not helping me more. I always seemed to be wondering why on earth he couldn't see my needs and meet them. And then God broke through.

God wanted me to see that Butch isn't the one who is to meet my needs. I am to turn to God and lean on Him. I kept piling onto Butch all my expectations, and he staggered under the weight because it was just too much of a burden for a human to carry. I also realized that I expected too much of myself. I realized I hated to seem weak or to fail to keep a commitment. It made me feel like a failure. That night, lying on the floor, I released Butch and myself from these unrealistic expectations.

God used this night of brokenness to refine Mandy. She says that this was a turning point in her growth as a Christian as she learned to truly trust God and to depend on Him. Walking in obedience to Christ has enabled her really to believe God's Word, which promises, "I can do all things through Him who strengthens me" (Philippians 4:13).

We can be sure that the intimacy of marriage will bring many chances to grow. We can resist the growth or welcome it knowing that in each trial God is lovingly shaping us to look more like Him. We can "exult in our tribulations, knowing that tribulation brings about perseverance; and perseverance, proven character; and proven character, hope; and hope does not disappoint, because the love of God has been poured out within our hearts through the Holy Spirit who was given to us" (Romans 5:3-5).

Covenant Love

God wants a Christian marriage to be a witness to a love radically different from the world's love. God's covenant love has no conditions, and He never takes it away. That's the same love we're to have in marriage. Without God, marriage ties are based on personal happiness and fickle commitment, but covenant love is a witness to others that God's love is everlasting.

Because God's love is everlasting, a covenant marriage is meant to

last "till death do us part." "Sadly too many times after couples have
verbalized a covenant relationship, they practice a contract marriage in
which giving is conditioned on the spouse's positive behavior."[1]

All the concepts of this book—being our husbands' helpers,
loving our husbands, submitting to our husbands, respecting our
husbands, choosing attitudes that build up rather than tear down our
husbands—describe ways to show the world a covenant marriage. A
covenant marriage always loves, always protects, and always believes
in the marriage. I heard of a man who joked, "If my wife leaves me,
I'm going with her!" When you're committed to a covenant marriage,
you have no place else to go except into one another's arms. I think
about Tina's incredible love in the previous chapter. What an example
of covenant love; what an example of God's love.

I hope that as you've read this book, prayed, and applied the
principles of being a godly wife, you've seen your marriage get better
and better. I pray that your marriage reflects the covenant love of our
heavenly Father.

Better Together

God designed marriage not only to be a witness to the world of
covenant love, but also to help a man and woman serve God together.
The vision you share with your husband helps you transcend the daily
grind. You are truly better together when you both commit to serving
God. Serving Him is the greatest adventure a Christian individual or
couple can ever know.

An Incredible Adventure

One of my favorite movies in recent years is *The Incredibles*. In it
we can find lessons about living an adventure with our family.

As the movie opens, the former superhero Mr. Incredible, now
known as Bob Parr, lives the suburban life with his wife, Helen, formerly
the superhero Elastigirl, and three kids, Dash, Violet, and Jack-Jack,
all of whom are also gifted with superpowers. Fifteen years earlier,
lawsuits by disgruntled people who they'd helped forced them to retire
their superhero powers and to live in anonymity. Their lives are now

marked by the mundane and routine. Helen seems to have adjusted fairly well as she builds a normal life with her family, but Bob's job as an insurance agent leaves him deflated and bored. He plods through life yearning for the good old days when he was a hero.

Hmmm…I wonder if my husband ever feels that way. Longing for the good old days when he was a superhero? Okay, not a superhero, but a man energized with purpose and passion.

Let's return to *The Incredibles*. One night while in his basement where he obviously spends time reminiscing, Bob is offered the opportunity to return to the life of a superhero. A mysterious woman named Mirage invites him to become Mr. Incredible once again and to save the world from a powerful machine called Kronos. Thinking he's returning to work for the government, Bob quickly agrees and in a hilarious scene dons his superhero suit once again to become Mr. Incredible.

The first lesson of *The Incredibles* is that a man needs to dream. Bob spends hours dreaming about his past and imagining being a superhero once again. Maybe our husbands can't return to the past, but can they include something from their dreams in their present lives? For example, basketball has always been a big part of my husband's life. Now he enjoys this passion by coaching our sons and helping to organize our community's youth leagues.

Does your husband share his dreams with you? His dreams are an integral part of who he is, and as he shares these dreams, you grow closer to each other.

Back to the movie. A problem arises when Bob doesn't tell Helen that he's returned to superhero work. While he pretends to go to his insurance job every day, we see him training for his new mission of conquering evil. As he returns to his former glory, he's excited about using his gifts, he's got a bounce in his step, and he's passionate for his wife, Helen, and for life. He's energized and ignited for life!

Energized. Passionate. Ignited. Do these words describe our husbands? Another lesson from the movie: A man needs an adventure! It makes him feel alive! Do you remember from the previous chapter that a man needs to know he has what it takes? An adventure is one of the things that make him feel he has what it takes. You may be thinking, *That's fine for the movies, but what kind of adventures can my husband live today? He has responsibilities like a job and a family. He can't just take off and do whatever he wants.* Well, no, but can't his responsibilities be part of the adventure?

My husband has many dreams for the future, and one of those is to incorporate his gift of encouragement with his love of coaching youth sports. He imagines how this could one day be a ministry at our church. This is a ministry that our whole family could be a part of. It's not my particular dream, but I can get excited about being a part of it. What about you? Does your husband have a dream he can share with you and the kids?

Back to *The Incredibles* one more time. Mr. Incredible eventually discovers that his adventures have been orchestrated by the villain Syndrome. Meanwhile, Helen discovers that Bob has returned to being Mr. Incredible. So she and her two older children become a part of the adventure when they reclaim their superpowers to save Bob and the world from Syndrome's evil schemes.

This is my favorite part of the movie! The entire family (except baby Jack-Jack) joins in the adventure! They have a wild ride as they each use their superpowers. They discover that each of their talents is needed. They can only be victorious by working together. They are better together.

Thus the third lesson of the movie: Live the adventure together! Are you willing to join your husband in an adventure? What might that adventure look like? Have you and your husband spent some time dreaming together, talking, and praying to be open to adventure?

Living the Adventure Together

David and Becky Peed are living an adventure they never would have imagined for their lives. Their willingness to join God in an adventure has enriched their lives, and they both say they're experiencing the abundant life God promises. Becky tells the story of the journey God has taken them on.

My husband and I played it safe for a long time, but we

both couldn't get past the nagging feeling that this was not the radical, abundant life Jesus promised. We both wanted that life but didn't know what to do about it. So we both prayed, *Here I am; use me!* God answered that prayer in a way we never would have imagined.

The journey that God has led us on this year is infinitely more than I would ever dare to have dreamed, asked, or hoped for. Our amazing blessings came to us from across the world when we adopted two Liberian orphan teenagers, Sam and Dora. With them they brought laughter and the sounds of big feet clamoring up the stairs. They brought belly laughs so deep you can't help but get tickled and a dialect we can sometimes hardly understand. They brought unsolicited hugs and pats that let me know I am special.

As we've lived the adventure together of adopting Sam and Dora, our marriage and family ties are stronger than ever. Our family life with five kids is sometimes crazy, but we love it! God has changed our perspective and view of life in ways we could have never imagined. We trust God daily as He directs our paths. We now view life as an adventure, and we never know what is around the next bend. Our well-ordered life is something of the past, and we never want to go back.

Our prayer is, *God, where do You want us to go next?* Our bags of faith and trust are packed, and we are excited to see what God has planned for us. We are experiencing what the Savior wants to give us.[2]

Serving Together

Serving God together can be a great adventure for you and your husband. Sometimes our fears threaten to keep us from joining God in the adventures He has planned for us. Becky and Dave also had fears, but they didn't let those fears rule them. As Dave explains, God was asking them to step out in faith.

After hearing the Liberian Boys Choir sing for the first time and learning that all of the boys in the choir needed to be adopted, Becky and I discussed what we thought God would have us do. In my quiet time, I read Luke 9—the account of Jesus feeding the 5000. "Late in the afternoon the twelve disciples came to him and said, 'Send the crowds away to the nearby villages and farms, so they can find food and lodging for the night. There is nothing to eat here in this deserted place.' " Jesus' response spoke directly to my heart as I was asking Him what we were to do about the orphans from Liberia. "But Jesus said, 'You feed them' " (Luke 9:13).

I prayed, *Lord, I don't know anything about raising teenagers from another country and culture, let alone orphans who have been through unbelievable hardship, but we want to follow You and completely surrender to Your will.* I felt as if the Lord said, *If you will trust Me, I will supply all you need to raise these children.*

As we have taken this step of faith, God has revealed Himself to us in ways that we would never have known. Our new life is not always easy, but we would never go back to the life we once knew.

Dave and Becky were afraid but realized that their faith could be stronger than their fears. Men and women of great faith were afraid too. The first thing the angel Gabriel told Mary when he explained to her that she would be the mother of Jesus was "do not be afraid" (Luke 1:30). Fear caused Moses to try to talk God out of calling him to lead the Israelites out of Egypt. And over and over God told Joshua to be strong and courageous.

God knows we might be fearful, but we can still step out in faith. God knows that having a partner in the adventure can give us courage. In our marriages we can draw strength and courage from one another and God. "A cord of three strands is not quickly torn apart" (Ecclesiastes 4:12).

We can use the excuse of fear to keep us from responding in obedience, or we can exercise faith to take a leap into God's arms. As John Ortberg states in his book *If You Want to Walk on Water, You've Got to Get Out of the Boat,* "I never want the no of fear to trump the yes of faith."[3] When we say yes in faith, we live the adventure with God that He intended for us.

We Are His Workmanship

God created us for a purpose and tells us He has a ministry prepared for us. "For we are His workmanship, created in Christ Jesus for good works, which God prepared beforehand so that we would walk in them" (Ephesians 2:10).

Marriage can actually be a training ground where we can refine our character and develop our spiritual gifts

> For many of us, at least a good portion of our adult lives will be spent in a marriage relationship. If we follow biblical guidelines for marriage, this relationship can enhance our growth as disciples of Christ. It can provide for us an opportunity to practice such principles as servanthood and unconditional love. But as Christians, we must remember that marriage is not an end in itself. Individually and as a couple, we are to give ourselves to ministering in our community and around the world.[4]

As we minister beyond our own home, we become to others the very heart, hands, and feet of Christ. Every believer has been given spiritual gifts to use for other people's benefit. "But to each one is given the manifestation of the Spirit for the common good" (1 Corinthians 12:7). Scott and I are so thankful for Southbrook Community Church, where we have learned about our spiritual gifts. Some of Scott's main gifts are leadership, giving, and service. He becomes alive when he's using these gifts for God! We have enjoyed seeing where God has led him to use those gifts in service.

What About Your Individual Ministry?

God loves you as an individual and has a specific calling for your life. As a wife, your first ministry is to your husband. Applying the principles we've discussed in this book is the ministry you can have to your husband. Remember that you are your husband's only wife, and only you can love him and minister to him as a wife. Ministering to your husband is one way to love God.

When considering a ministry beyond the home front, I encourage you to find a way you and your husband can serve together. That might mean being your husband's helper in whatever he's called to do.

> Whatever God has called your husband to be or do, He has also called you to support it and be a part of it, if in no other way than to pray, encourage, and help in whatever way possible. For some women that means creating a good home, raising the children, being there for him, and offering prayer support. Other women may take an active role by becoming a partner or helper. In either case, God does not ask you to deny your personhood in the process. God has called you to something, too. But it will fit in with whatever your husband's calling is, it will not be in conflict with it. God is not the author of confusion, strife or unworkable situations. He is a God of perfect timing. There is a time for everything, the Bible says. The timing to do what God has called each of you to do will work out perfectly, if it's submitted to God.[5]

Also, keep in mind that in some seasons in your life, you will need to focus your time and energy on your family and serve only in smaller ways beyond your home. Later, when the kids are older, you might be called to serve in a larger role somewhere outside the home. But keep your priorities in order. If you are serving individually, make sure you have your husband's blessing on whatever you do. God will bless your desire to honor your husband.

Packing Your Bags for Adventure

Becky and Dave's story inspires me to look for God's leading for an adventure my husband and I can share. Becky said that their "bags of faith, belief, and trust are packed." Are your bags packed for an adventure? What might the adventure of serving God look like for you and your husband? Becky and Dave's adventure included adopting two Liberian teenagers. Other couples might reach out to neighbors or lead a small group. Teaching Sunday school, going on a missions trip, giving financially, or working in a homeless shelter are some other ideas. The world is so full of hurts and needs, and you can easily find a way to serve the Lord by loving others.

I encourage you to pray for a way that you and your husband can serve together. You'll please the Lord, defeat the schemes of the enemy, and increase your spiritual intimacy with your husband at the same time.

PRAYER GUIDE

Dear Jesus,

I pray that our marriage will reflect Your purposes and bring You glory as we show one another covenant love. May our love not be conditional, and may we be committed to this marriage "till death do us part." Give us hearts to serve one another and then to look beyond our own doors to serve others. Show us an adventure we can go on together, and may that adventure be about You, not about ourselves. Let us find joy and excitement in serving You, Lord, in Jesus' name. Amen.

Epilogue

At the beginning of this book I asked you some questions to see if you were ready to let God transform your marriage. Now I want to ask you some questions so you can reflect on where you've come in your marriage journey.

What thoughts do you think your husband has of you as his wife? Would he say you're his helper? His partner? His lover? Do you love him, submit to him, and respect him? Do you show him attitudes that open his heart to you? Do you forgive him the way Christ forgives you? Would he say you treasure his friendship most in the world? What do you think God thinks about the way you live out your role as a wife?

As I wrote earlier in the book, I am a work in progress, and my marriage is too. Writing this book has been a gift from God that has both delighted me and challenged me. Our greatest joy is to be used by God, but that is sometimes also our greatest challenge. I am sure that one of the reasons God called me to write this particular book was so that I would seek Him for my own marriage.

In the process of writing I've been reminded that my primary purpose for seeking Jesus is not to make my marriage turn out exactly the way I want it. Not at all. I've been reminded that Jesus Himself is the reward I'm seeking. Through this journey I've fallen more in love with the Lord and more in love with my husband. As I've followed in the footsteps of Jesus to apply His ways in my marriage, I've discovered two gifts: the richness of a closer relationship with the Lord and the treasure of a marriage lived God's way. Can you say you've discovered the same gifts? My hope and prayer is that you can.

Read this beautiful story of enduring love and let the words of the husband settle in your heart.

> My parents fell in love at first sight, and they've been in love for more than fifty-two years. They're not just comfortable with each other, or merely tolerant of each other's faults. They are still truly, deeply in love, with all the passion and heartache that wildly emotional state entails.
>
> My father has always been more of a tease than a romantic, and he has regaled us with tales of his exploits all our lives. For example, the first time he and my mother ever spoke to each other was after World War II, after Daddy had just returned from Japan. He was driving his brother's brand-new car through town when he saw my mother go into a furniture store. Pulling over, he jumped out of the car and managed to slip into the store right behind her. My twenty-six-year-old mother, who was thinking about finding an apartment, asked the store owner to show her a twin bedroom set she had admired the week before. My father, a mere passing acquaintance, stepped up beside her and said, "Now Maude, we are not sleeping on twin beds."
>
> They were married three months later, and they did sleep on one of the twin beds until they could afford a double bed.
>
> At age seventy-eight, my father had open-heart surgery. My seventy-six-year-old mother spent every night at the hospital, and every day beside his bed. The first thing Daddy said when they removed the tracheal tube from his throat was one of the most

romantic things I've ever heard. He said, "Maude, you know what that doctor found when he cut me open? He found your name engraved on my heart."[1]

Oh, how I want my name to be engraved on my husband's heart. What about you? Whatever condition your marriage is in now, I hope you will press on, taking one step at a time, following the footsteps of Jesus toward the beautiful and satisfying marriage He wants you to have.

I hope the end of this book finds you treasuring the gift of the husband God has given you. And as you treasure him with a thankful heart, may your love for Jesus and for your husband fill you to overflowing. May your husband say about you what God says in Proverbs 18:22: "He who finds a wife finds a good thing and obtains favor from the LORD."

Study Guide

Chapter 1—Pour Out Your Heart to God

1. Before you continue to read this book, consider making these commitments:

   - First, commit to pursuing God. Spend time with God every day. Praise God, confess your sins, thank God for His blessings, and pray for God to reveal His truth.

   - Second, commit to looking honestly at yourself and your ways (not your husband's).

   - Third, commit to looking to Scripture to see what God says about marriage.

   - Fourth, commit to applying the lessons God reveals to you through these pages.

- Last, commit to praying *daily* for your husband and your marriage.

  Please sign and date your commitment to these action steps.

  Signature _____ Date_____

2. What do you hope to gain from reading this book?

3. What are your dreams for you and your husband 10 years from now? 20? 30? 40?

4. What character traits do you see in your own life that are helpful to your marriage? What traits do you have that hinder your marriage? Read Romans 2:4. Ask God to show you what you need to confess.

5. Have you surrendered your marriage to God? What reservations do you have about surrendering your marriage to God? What changes will that entail?

6. "Trust GOD from the bottom of your heart; don't try to figure out everything on your own. Listen for GOD's voice in everything you do, everywhere you go; he's the One who will keep you on track. Don't assume that you know it all. Run to GOD! Run from evil!" (Proverbs 3:5-7 MSG).

   - With what attitude do we need to approach God?

   - List specific actions these verses tell you to take.

   - What's the benefit of trusting God?

7. Read Matthew 7:24-25.

   - God is the Rock. What does that mean to you?

   - Find other verses that refer to God as our Rock and record them in your notebook.

8. Read John 15:5.

   - What does abiding in Christ mean?

- How do you abide in Christ?

- Why does God want us to abide in Christ?

9. Read and write out Colossians 1:17. How does this verse apply to your marriage?

10. Read and write out Colossians 4:2. Write down three specific things about your husband for which you're thankful. Mention these in a prayer of thanksgiving to God.

11. Pretend your marriage is a garden. In what ways are you treating your husband like a weed? In what ways are you treating him like a flower?

12. Think of one thing you can say today to make your husband feel your love for him. Write it in your notebook.

13. Plan to take at least one specific action this week to make your husband know he is a priority to you. Write your plan of action in your notebook.

14. Read Psalm 62:8.

- What two actions does this verse tell us to take?

- What does the fact that "God is a refuge" mean to you?

15. In your journal write down a prayer in which you pour out your heart to God about your husband and your marriage.

Chapter 2—Start with Jesus

1. Read Matthew 6:33.

- What does this verse say about priorities?

- What promise does it give?

- How might you more effectively follow the guidelines of this verse in your own life?

2. Read Psalm 46:10.

- Why do you think God gave us this commandment?

- How can you practice this commandment today?

3. List in order at least five of your priorities. Do you think these are the priorities God wants you to have? Do you think they're in the correct order?

4. List three practical steps you can take to establish a daily quiet time.

5. Write down what each letter of the ACTS acronym means.

6. Use the following verses to apply the ACTS model of prayer.

   A—Psalm 150:6

   C—Acts 3:19

   T—1 Thessalonians 5:16-18

   S—Matthew 19:26

7. Read Romans 6:23.

   • Are you sure of your salvation?

   • When did you pray to receive Christ?

8. Read Psalm 119, which focuses on God's Word. Record what each of the verses listed below says about God's Word and about a person who loves God's Word.

   • verse 2

   • verse 11

   • verse 45

   • verse 103

   • verse 105

   • verse 130

   • verse 165

9. Have you ever memorized Scripture? As you do this study, I encourage you to memorize Scripture verses that will be a help to you in your marriage.

10. Read 1 Peter 3:1-4. What kind of behavior will win your husband to the Lord?

11. Read 1 Peter 3:8. According to this verse, how does God want you to treat your husband?

12. Do you and your husband pray together? Have you told God this is something you'd like to do with your husband? Have you asked God to give your husband the desire? Have you ever asked your husband to pray with you? What steps will you take this week?

13. Read the commitment statement you signed in the study guide for chapter 1. How are you doing?

Chapter 3—What Is a Helper?

1. Review the commitment to action steps you signed in the study guide for chapter 1. How are you doing?

2. Read Deuteronomy 30:11. Rephrase this promise in your own words.

3. Read Ephesians 2:10.

    • What are we called? What does this word mean?

    • What we were created for?

    • What does this verse mean for marriage?

4. Read Psalm 139:23-24. Ask God to examine your heart and reveal any wrong expectations you're placing on your husband.

5. Read and write down 2 Timothy 1:7.

    • How can this verse help you in your marriage?

    • Do you have any fears that are keeping you from being your husband's helper?

6. You read about three aspects of being your husband's helper. Which is the easiest for you? Which is the most challenging?

7. Do you think your husband thinks of you as his helper? Explain.

8. List one specific thing you can do to develop your friendship with your husband.

9. Have you been unwilling to do something you know your husband

has wanted you to do for him? Will you pray for God to help you do that one thing this week?

10. How's your attitude about sex? If you've been reluctant, pray for God to renew your desire.

11. Are you content in your role as your husband's helper?

12. What's the difference between a role and an identity?

13. Read Colossians 2:8. What lies might be preventing you from enjoying your marriage?

14. Pray for God to show you one specific way you can be your husband's helper this week. Write it down, promise God you'll do it, and then put it into action!

15. Have you had a quiet time using the ACTS model?

Chapter 4—A Heart of Love

1. In chapter 3 we discussed loving your husband by being his friend. List a few ways you've been a friend to your husband.

2. In this chapter we've learned about three types of love: romantic, sexual, and unconditional. Which type of love is the most challenging for you to show your husband? Why?

3. Have you ever talked to your husband about your sex life? Do you think you need to?

4. Read Hebrews 13:4. What do you learn in this verse?

5. Read 1 Corinthians 7:3-5. Summarize Paul's teaching about sex in these verses.

6. Use the suggestions from this chapter (or create one of your own) to show your husband romantic and/or physical love. Try being creative, surprising, adventuresome, or mysterious. Write down your plan and promise God you'll do it this week.

7. Read 1 John 3:1. What does being a child of God mean to you?

8. Read 1 John 4:19. In what way does God's love for us enable us to love others?

9. Read 1 Peter 4:8. How does this verse apply to your marriage?

10. Read Ephesians 4:32.

- What is our best motivation for forgiving our husbands?

- List one way you can follow each of the commands in this verse this week.

11. Are you holding a grudge, keeping score, or harboring bitterness against your husband? If so, what do you need to forgive your husband for? Have you asked for God's forgiveness? Have you asked for your husband's forgiveness?

12. Read Colossians 3:12-17.

- List the guidelines for godly living in this verse.

- Verse 14 says to "put on love." List a few practical ways you can do this.

13. Read John 13:3-5. What are some modern-day equivalents of washing someone's feet?

14. In what ways have you served your husband in love? In what ways have you sacrificed for your husband in love?

15. Review the commitment statement you signed in the study guide for chapter 1. How are you doing?

Chapter 5—The Two Biggies: Submission and Respect

1. Read the following verses and write down the benefits of waiting on the Lord.

- Psalm 27:14

- Psalm 40:1-3

2. What does "waiting on the Lord" mean? What do waiting on the Lord and submitting to your husband have to do with each other?

3. Read the following verses and write down what you learn about submission.

- James 4:7

- 2 Chronicles 30:8

- Deuteronomy 11:26-32

4. List some areas on your life in which the Lord is asking you to submit to Him.

5. Read Romans 8:5-6.

   - How do we walk in the flesh? In the Spirit?

   - What's the result of walking in the flesh? In the Spirit?

   - How can we walk in the Spirit in marriage?

6. Read Colossians 3:17.

   - What does this verse say we can do for the Lord?

   - What attitude does God want us to have when we do things for Him?

7. Describe a time when you submitted to your husband. How can you submit to your husband now?

8. Do you think you've believed any lies about submission? Summarize God's perspective of submission.

9. "However, let each man of you love...his wife as...his very own self; and let the wife see that she respects and reverences her husband [that she notices him, regards him, honors him, prefers him, venerates, and esteems him; and that she defers to him, praises him, and loves and admires him exceedingly]" (Ephesians 5:33 AMP).

   - Which words stand out to you?

   - Which of the above actions do you think would mean the most to your husband?

10. What do you think about the idea of unconditional respect of your husband? Do you practice this in your marriage?

11. Read Proverbs 3:27. How can you put this verse into practice in your marriage?

12. What specific thing can you do or say to show your husband unconditional respect?

13. Read Galatians 6:9. What encouragement does this verse offer you?

14. What are you sowing into your marriage? What are you reaping in your marriage?

15. Have you prayed for your husband today?

Chapter 6—Attitude Adjustment

1. List the seven attitudes discussed in this chapter.

   • Which of these attitudes is the easiest for you to show your husband?

   • Which of these attitudes is the most difficult for you to show your husband? Why?

2. Have any other attitudes come to mind that your husband needs from you?

3. Read Galatians 5:22-23.

   • What fruit is evident in your marriage?

   • What fruit would you like to see increase?

   • How can you cooperate with God to see that happen?

4. Read John 15:5.

   • What does "abiding in Christ" mean to you?

   • What's the result of abiding?

5. Which of the attitudes in this chapter do you think your husband needs you to focus on? Choose one attitude to pray about, think about, and put into practice in your marriage. Write it down.

6. Read the following translations of Proverbs 4:23:

>   Watch over your heart with all diligence,
>   for from it flow the springs of life.

>Above all else, guard your heart,
>for it is the wellspring of life (NIV).

>Keep vigilant watch over your heart;
>*that's* where life starts (MSG).

- What does "guard your heart" mean?

- What comes out of our hearts?

- In what ways can you guard your heart for the sake of your marriage?

7. Think of someone who exhibits some of the attitudes discussed in this chapter. How does that person affect you?

8. Read Matthew 7:1-5.

- How does judgment affect your marriage?

- What do these verses tell us about judging others?

9. Read the following verses. How can the lessons of these verses help your marriage?

- Philippians 4:13

- Luke 18:27

10. Are the attitudes you show your husband more like fragrant flowers or stinky garbage? Explain.

11. Read 1 Thessalonians 5:21. What are the good things in your marriage to hold on to? Do you need to let go of anything?

12. Read and write down Proverbs 18:22. Can your husband say this about you?

13. Are you staying in touch with God throughout the day by praying?

Chapter 7—Help for the Helper

1. Read John 7:37-38. What are you tempted to turn to when you're thirsty? How can you let Jesus quench your thirst?

2. In what ways is the Holy Spirit your Helper?

   • John 14:26

   • 1 Corinthians 2:10

   • Philippians 2:1

3. What two lessons does Debbie's story offer us (page 109)? What do you think about her advice? How can you apply it to your situation?

4. In the study guide for chapter 2, I asked you to write down your top five priorities. Review them—has anything changed? What might God think about your priorities?

5. Is anything in your life preventing you from making God your top priority? Is anything in your life keeping you from making your husband your second priority? Does your husband feel that he's a priority to you?

6. What have you done lately just for fun? If you had several hours to refresh your spirit, what would you do? Ask God to give you time for this activity.

7. Do you think you would be selfish if you did something just for you?

8. Read Proverbs 11:1. What insight does this verse give you about the various roles and responsibilities in your life?

9. Do your friendships help or hinder your marriage?

10. Write down the three action steps to take to prevent stinkin' thinkin'.

11. Ask God to reveal any lies you're believing about your husband or your marriage. Write those down. Then write down a truth you can replace the lie with.

12. Read Philippians 4:8-9. What specific things can you think about that meet these criteria?

13. Does God want you to remove anything from your life or add anything to it to guard your thoughts?

14. How do the following verses relate to what you've learned about replacing lies with truth?

    - Romans 12:2

    - 2 Corinthians 10:5

    - Isaiah 43:18-21

    - John 8:32

    - Proverbs 23:7

15. Are you having a daily quiet time with the Lord?

Chapter 8—Hearts at Home

1. What is your reaction to Suzie's story at the beginning of the chapter?

2. Based on what you read, what is a homemaker?

3. In Titus 2:3-5, we're told to do certain things, one of which is to be a worker at home, "so that the word of God will not be dishonored." How can being a homemaker bring honor to God? What about homemaking would dishonor God?

4. How do you feel about being a worker at home?

5. How are you doing at being at home? Do you think this is an important part of being a homemaker?

6. Is idleness keeping you from your responsibilities at home? Is busyness keeping you from your responsibilities at home?

7. Read Psalm 127:1. How might you apply this verse to your home?

8. Read Psalm 127:3. Do you treasure your children as gifts from the Lord?

9. Would your husband say you are content as a mother? Does he usually hear you enjoying your children or complaining about them?

10. In what ways are you and your husband operating as a parenting team?

11. Ask your husband if he wants to talk about priorities in your parenting. If he doesn't want to talk, don't get mad! Write down your top three priorities in your notebook. Share these with your husband.

12. Read Deuteronomy 6:4-9. What do you learn in these verses about what to teach your children?

13. Is your husband assured that he is a priority before the kids? Does he see this in your words, attitude, and actions?

14. Read Proverbs 14:1. In what ways are you a wise woman at home? In what ways have you acted like a foolish woman?

15. Pray for God to show you something specific today that will help you to be your husband's helper at home.

16. Have you been praying for your husband each day?

Chapter 9—Accepting Your Man

1. How have you applied God's command to "leave and cleave" in your own marriage? What parts have been easy, and what parts have been difficult?

2. Would your husband say that he can completely trust in your allegiance to him?

3. What is the difference between a bride and a wife?

4. What differences between you and your husband tend to irritate you? What differences delight you? How can the way you think about these differences turn the irritations into positives?

5. What can you say or do to communicate to your husband that you embrace his uniqueness?

6. Read Proverbs 12:4. Have you ever made your husband feel ashamed or wrong for being different from you?

7. How does the concept of stinkin' thinkin' from the previous chapter relate to differences between you and your husband?

8. Read Ecclesiastes 3:7. Pray for God's wisdom about the amount of talking you do and the kind of talking you do. What did God bring

to mind? Does God want you to make any changes, especially when communicating with your husband?

9. How can the guidelines in James 1:19 help you communicate with your husband?

10. Read Romans 15:7. What are we told to do? How can acceptance give glory to God?

11. What are some differences between you and your husband when it comes to sex? Have you prayed about these differences? Have you talked to your husband about sex? Are you willing to love your husband by responding to him sexually?

12. Have you initiated sex? Have you brought passion and playfulness to the marriage bed? Review some of the ideas listed in chapter 4. Try one!

13. What lies might you be tempted to believe about sex that could prevent you from fully enjoying sex? Pray about this.

14. Review your commitment statement in the study guide for chapter 1. How are you doing?

Chapter 10—Surviving the Storms

1. Have you weathered a storm in your marriage? How did it affect your marriage?

2. Read each of the following verses. Write down the promises God gives you for going through hard times.

   • Exodus 14:13

   • Psalm 40:1-3

   • Isaiah 43:1-2

   • Romans 8:38

   • Psalm 37:23

   • Proverbs 10:25

3. Read Romans 5:3-5. What results have tribulations produced in your own life?

4. What seemingly impossible situation are you facing? How might God fulfill His promise in Matthew 19:26?

5. During stressful times, do you and your husband stand strongly together, or do you tend to turn against one another?

6. Read Galatians 6:2.

   • How can you love and support your husband during a stressful time?

   • List some practical words you can say and actions you can take this week.

7. What does an eternal perspective include? How can this help you during a storm?

8. What is your reaction to Tina and Steve's story?

9. How do you guard your heart against unfaithfulness?

10. In this chapter I wrote, "Times of brokenness in our marriage can be the very experiences that shape us and cause us to enjoy the sweetest fellowship with the Lord and with each other that we'll ever know." Respond to this statement.

11. Read Psalm 66:10-12. Meditate on the beauty of these promises.

Chapter 11—Better Than Ever, Better Together

1. Read James 4:7-8.

   • How might you follow these commands in your marriage?

   • What blessings might you experience by applying these commands to your marriage?

2. Have conflicts with your husband ever kept you from serving God?

3. Read Malachi 2:14. God says that the wife is a "companion" and "your wife by covenant." How does this relate to Malachi 2:16?

4. Read Matthew 19:6. What is the value of knowing that God has

joined you to your husband? What does the phrase "one flesh" mean to you?

5. Read Genesis 17:1-9. What are the conditions and the blessings of the covenant between God and Abraham?

6. What are some of the principles of covenant love?

7. Is your marriage a witness to the world of covenant love?

8. Read John 13:34-35.

   • What is new about Jesus' commandment?

   • How does following this commandment show others we are Jesus' disciples?

9. Read John 9:4. Jesus said that He did the "the works of Him who sent Me." What guidelines does this offer you in serving God?

10. Read 1 Corinthians 3:9-15. Describe the kind of work that will last eternally.

11. Does your husband share his dreams with you? Do you encourage him to? Do you support your husband's dreams with your attitude and actions?

12. What adventure of serving God could you and your husband share right now? What adventures could you share in the future? I encourage you to take time to talk and dream with your husband about ministries you can participate in together.

13. Read Ephesians 2:10. As a wife, where does God want your main ministry to be? In what ways are you living this out in your life?

14. Read Philippians 2:13. How can you apply this promise to your marriage?

15. Have you been praying throughout the day? Have you been having daily quiet times?

Epilogue

1. Read James 1:17. List some of the reasons your marriage is one of the good things given to you from God.

2. Read Hebrews 12:1-2. What encumbrance or sin do you need to set aside in your marriage?

3. Read 2 Corinthians 5:17 and Revelation 21:5. In what ways has God made your marriage new?

4. Has your marriage changed from reading and applying the principles in this book? In what ways?

5. List two or three things you want to take away from reading this book.

Notes

Chapter 1—Pour Out Your Heart to God

1. Anabel Gillham, *The Confident Woman: Knowing Who You Are in Christ* (Eugene, OR: Harvest House Publishers, 1993), pp. 37-38.

Chapter 2—Start with Jesus

1. Sharon Jaynes, *Becoming a Woman Who Listens to God* (Eugene, OR: Harvest House Publishers, 2004), p. 10.

2. Cynthia Heald, *A Woman's Journey to the Heart of God* (Nashville: Thomas Nelson Publishers, 1997), p. 15.

Chapter 3—What Is a Helper?

1. Shaunti Feldhahn, *For Women Only* (Sisters, OR: Multnomah Publishers, 2004), p. 147.

2. Elizabeth George, *A Woman After God's Own Heart* (Eugene, OR: Harvest House Publishers, 1997), p. 127.

3. Mike Mason, *The Mystery of Marriage* (Sisters, OR: Multnomah Publishers, 1985), p. 103.

Chapter 4—A Heart of Love

1. Shaunti Feldhahn, *For Women Only* (Sisters, OR: Multnomah Publishers, 2004), p. 139.

2. Chuck and Nancy Missler, *The Way of Agape* (Coeur d'Alene, ID: Koinonia House, 1994) p.46.

3. Rick Warren, *Better Together: What on Earth Are We Here For?* (Lake Forest, CA: PurposeDriven, 2004), p. 16.

4. Gary Chapman, *Covenant Marriage* (Nashville: Broadman & Holman Publishers, 2003), p. 28.

5. Stormie Omartian, *The Power of a Praying Wife* (Eugene, OR: Harvest House Publishers, 1997), p. 31.

Chapter 5—The Two Biggies: Submission and Respect

1. Neil T. Anderson, *The Bondage Breaker* (Eugene, OR: Harvest House Publishers, 1990), pp. 45-46.

2. Emerson Eggerichs, *Motivating Your Man God's Way* (Grand Rapids, MI: Love and Respect Ministries, Inc., 2002), p. 30.

3. Shaunti Feldhahn, *For Women Only* (Sisters, OR: Multnomah Publishers, 2004), p. 39.

4. Nancy Cobb and Connie Grigsby, *The Politically Incorrect Wife* (Sisters, OR: Multnomah Publishers, 2000), p. 106.

Chapter 6—Attitude Adjustment

1. Lysa TerKeurst, *Capture His Heart* (Chicago: Moody Press, 2002), p. 67.

2. Lysa TerKeurst, "Is This Your Greatest Day Ever?" *Proverbs 31 Woman,* August 2001, p. 1.

3. Renee Swope, "He Knows the Plans," *Encouragement for Today,* proverbs31 .gospelcom.net, June 20, 2005.

4. Nancy Leigh DeMoss, *Lies Women Believe and the Truth That Sets Them Free* (Chicago: Moody Press, 2001), p. 194.

5. Christopher L. Burge and Pamela Toussaint, *His Rules* (Colorado Springs: Waterbrook Press, 2005), p. 174.

6. John Eldredge, *Wild at Heart* (Nashville: Thomas Nelson Publishers, 2001), p. 9.

7. Ibid., p. 46.

8. Elizabeth George, *A Woman after God's Own Heart* (Eugene, OR: Harvest House Publishers, 1997), p. 93.

Chapter 7—Help for the Helper

1. Denise George, *Come to the Quiet* (Minneapolis: Bethany House Publishers, 2003), p. 21.
2. Joyce Meyer, *Battlefield of the Mind* (Tulsa: Harrison House, Inc., 1995), pp. 15-16.

Chapter 8—Hearts at Home

1. Pat Ennis and Lisa Tatlock, interviewed by Nancy Leigh DeMoss, "Home-making Is Not a Dirty Word," www.reviveourhearts.com, July 13, 2004.
2. Jean Fleming, *A Mother's Heart* (Colorado Springs: NavPress, 1982), p. 45.
3. Karen Rinehart, *Invisible Underwear, Bus Stop Mommies, and Other Things True To Life* (Baltimore: PublishAmerica, 2003), pp. 31-32.

Chapter 9—Accepting Your Man

1. Florence Littauer, *Personality Plus for Couples* (Grand Rapids, MI: Fleming H. Revell, 2001), p. 19.
2. Gary Chapman, *Covenant Marriage* (Nashville: Broadman & Holman Publishers, 2003), p. 36.
3. Bill and Pam Farrel, *Men Are Like Waffles—Women Are Like Spaghetti* (Eugene, OR: Harvest House Publishers, 2001), p. 11.
4. Ibid., p. 13.
5. Tim Alan Gardner, *Sacred Sex* (Colorado Springs: WaterBrook Press, 2002), p. 101.
6. Shaunti Feldhahn, *For Women Only* (Sisters, OR: Multnomah Publishers, 2004), p. 107.
7. Gardner, p. 196.

Chapter 10—Surviving the Storms

1. John Eldredge, *Wild at Heart* (Nashville: Thomas Nelson Publishers, 2001), p. 18.
2. Shaunti Feldhahn, *For Women Only* (Sisters, OR: Multnomah Publishers, 2004), p. 68.

Chapter 11—Better Than Ever, Better Together

1. Gary Chapman, *Covenant Marriage* (Nashville: Broadman & Holman Publishers, 2003), p. 17.
2. For information about Liberian adoptions or information about supporting the Liberian orphanage, please contact David and Becky Peed at peedd@yahoo.com.
3. John Ortberg, *If You Want to Walk on Water, You've Got to Get Out of the Boat* (Grand Rapids, MI: Zondervan, 2001), p. 119.

4. Chapman, p. 4.

5. Stormie Omartian, *The Power of a Praying Wife* (Eugene, OR: Harvest House Publishers, 1997), p. 95.

Epilogue

1. Told by Rickey Mallory, *Chicken Soup for the Romantic Soul,* ed. Jack Canfield et al. (Deerfield Beach, FL: Health Communications, Inc., 2002), pp. 81-82.

Acknowledgments

~⌒~

To my husband, Scott. You are my greatest treasure.

To my sons, Zachary and Tyler. You are the greatest evidence in my life of God's love for me.

To my parents, for nurturing an early love of the written word and for lovingly supporting me through the years.

To my dear friends Amy, Catherine, Holly, Karen, and Kelly. Thank you for listening to me, praying for me, and laughing with me.

To Scott, Natalie, and Donna, for your friendship and love.

To the many men and women who shared their hearts and stories in this book.

To Proverbs 31 Ministries, and especially to Lysa, Glynnis, Renee, and Marybeth, for your example and support.

To my church home, Southbrook Community Church, for helping me to mature in the Lord.

To Harvest House Publishers, for making my dream come true.

Melanie Chitwood is a writer, teacher, and speaker living with her husband and two sones in Charlotte, North Carolina. To contact her for speaking engagements, visit her website and blog at melaniechitwood.com or contact Proverbs 31 Ministries at proverbs31.org. You can also e-mail Melanie at melandtheboys@gmail.com.

Other Great Harvest House Reading

What a Wife Needs from Her Husband
Melanie Chitwood

Building on the success of *What a Husband Needs from His Wife* (more than 30,000 copies sold), Melanie turns the tables and offers husbands practical ways they can love their wives more effectively and build successful marriages.

The Power of a Praying® Wife
Stormie Omartian

Stormie Omartian shares how you can develop a deeper relationship with your husband by praying for him. Packed with practical advice on praying for specific areas, including decision-making, fears, spiritual strength, and sexuality, this book will help you discover the fulfilling marriage God intended.

A Wife After God's Own Heart
Elizabeth George

One secret to marital bliss is for you to love your husband the way God designed you to love him. The rewards for doing so are rich! Examines 12 insights for a more fulfilling marriage.

Becoming the Woman of His Dreams
Sharon Jaynes

You'll love this thoughtful look at the wonderful, unique, and God-ordained role a woman has in her husband's life. Sharon Jaynes offers seven key qualities every wife should strive for.

Men Are Like Waffles—Women Are Like Spaghetti
Bill and Pam Farrel

Men keep life elements in separate boxes; women intertwine everything. Providing biblical insights, sound research, and humorous anecdotes, the Farrels explore gender differences and preferences and how they can strengthen relationships.